# The Cosmic Ballgame

## What 2012 and Mayan Creation Mean for Us

by

**David Miller**

ISBN # 978-0-615-54240-9

# Contents

# Acknowledgments

This book has been a lifetime in the making from the ball fields of my childhood to the ritual dances with the sun and moon as an adult. I owe a debt to all the ballplayers and ritual cosmic dancers that have touched my life.

In particular, I thank Starhawk for her unflagging support through traveling, writing and critiquing. I thank my daughters Juanita, Skye, Amie and Juliana for indulging my explanations. Juanita suffered especially when her dinner guests at home would ask what I was writing about and a lengthy discussion of ballgames ensued.

Over the years my circle brothers patiently persevered in listening to my ballgame theories. Magic Brook, Jim, and Dress stayed the longest on the course while Stephen, Michael, Karl, Daniel, and Rabbit also ran. Thanks guys.

Many thanks to Joe Johnston for the early introduction to Mayan painters and the connection for the cover art.

# The Cosmic Ballgame

Ballgames are important because they re-enact Creation.

The ancient Mayan Cosmic Ballgame re-enacted Creation through a sacrificial blood ballgame played over and over within Great Cycles. In playing the ballgame, Mayan shaman kings controlled the creative magic of blood and the power of time. In a similar vein, the modern ballgames of baseball, football, and basketball also re-enact Creation while harnessing the energy of blood and the flow of time.

The Mayan Cosmic Ballgame is important for us because it provides a portal, a better way to understand the symbolism in modern ballgames. Peering into the looking glass of Mayan shamans playing ball, we should be able to discern the future shape of present day shamans playing our ballgames of Creation.

In Mayan reckoning, we humans live in the Fourth Creation of the Great Cycles inaugurated by the Gods.

The First Creation saw the birth of animals on earth. But the animals could only shriek and not honor the Gods. The Second Creation failed because when the Gods attempted to make the "human work", they used mud. The mud people simply dissolved. The Third Creation also collapsed into disarray. The Gods had made wooden manikins for the human work. But the manikins had no thoughts. They multiplied but spoke gibberish and could not honor the Gods. Monkeys are the remnant of the Third Creation. Finally, in the Fourth Creation, humans were made from maize. This human work spoke clearly, successfully counted the days, and nurtured the Gods with blood sacrifice.

As they counted and named the days, the Mayans developed a brilliant calendar system: the 260 day lunar "Tzolkin", the 360+5 day solar "Haab", and the "Calendar Round" of 52 solar years. The Long Count calendar was a later development that established a more linear aspect to time to serve the political/historical needs of Mayan kings. It could stretch time in a straight path for thousands of years either into the past or the future. Shortly, the auspicious Long Count date of 13.0.0.0.0 4 Ajaw 8 Kumk'u (21 December 2012) concludes the Fourth Creation. Will a Fifth Creation begin?

The Classic Period Mayan kings lived and divined by their calendars which guided the performance of large public rituals and daily personal rituals. Time, within the framework of their calendars, was the container, the form of their life. But the substance of their lives was blood. Beneath the surface, beneath the veneer of time, beneath the illusion of time lay the realm of blood. Blood was the "mortar" of Mayan Creation, its driving force. And the sacrificial blood ballgame was the vehicle.

Fortunately, there is a place to discover the meaning of the Mayan blood ballgame. That place is a book. The book is called Popol Vuh or Council Book. Although the Popol Vuh was written in the 16th century CE in the K'iche Highlands of Guatemala, it is generally regarded to be a close reflection of Mayan Creation mythology from the early centuries BCE to the present, and geographically from the jungle lowlands to the mountain highlands.

The protagonists of the Popol Vuh are the Hero Twins, the "boys". They are named Hun-Ahpu and Xbalanque. With the fate of the universe on the line, with the dawn of Creation in the balance, the boys descend into the bowels of the Underworld, into Xibalba, where they play ball against the Lords of Death, rulers of this domain. The odds do not favor the boys. This is the turf, the home court of the Lords of Death. They are merciless. They already performed ballgame sacrifice upon One Hun-Ahpu, father of the boys. Little wonder Grandmother wept to see the boys follow their father's path.

But as one might expect, the boys prevailed over the Lords of Death. No trial, trick or voracious animal proved too much for the boys. After vanquishing the Lords of Death, the boys went to the Place of Ballgame Sacrifice to raise the bones of their father and establish him as First Father/Maize God. Then the boys ascended to the sky. When the sun rose, when it dawned for those born in the light, the first humans, the boys were there in the sky. One was sun, the other moon.

The Popol Vuh is a fantastic and wonderful story. Frankly, it is very entertaining and often humorous. But it is a serious tale. And the meaning that lies under the surface is our goal because the underlying purpose of the sacrificial blood ballgame is to usurp the blood magic of Blood Moon and the sacred count of days of Grandmother Time. The rubber ball in the blood ballgame is a symbol, a substitute for the heart of Blood Moon. She birthed the universe, the Hero Twins. The power of Grandmother Time resides in her 260 day Tzolkin. The cycles of human gestation, the phases of the moon, and the growing cycle of maize are the building blocks of the Tzolkin. The Gods, First Father, and the Hero Twins play the sacrificial blood ballgame with magical powers taken from Blood Moon and Grandmother.

Later, on earth, kings will re-enact the heroic deeds and dances of First Father and the Hero Twins as described in the Popol Vuh. In so doing, each divine king controls the Cosmic Ballgame of life and death, his kingdom, and time. The true purpose of the Popol Vuh, as the myth comes down to us, is to spin the story of Creation to support the Mayan kingship system. To understand the Popol Vuh, especially the sacrificial blood ballgame at its core, will be to understand the significance of 2012, which in essence is a turning point, a pause in the Cosmic Ballgame cycle before a resumption of the game.

Then, as an added attraction, at no extra cost, one Cosmic Ballgame will lead to another. The unparalleled gift I found in the Popol Vuh was the insight it gave me into modern ballgame culture. For every player of baseball, football and basketball knows in their bones that they are engaged in a Cosmic Ballgame dance that usurps the symbols of nature and time for use in a competitive warrior ballgame culture. The universal story of Creation is re-enacted in our ballgames season upon season as shaman ballplayers guide us through the cycles of birth, life, death, and rebirth.

I'm ahead of myself, though.

Since there is a journey in every tale, let me return to my travels to Tikal and Copan, when I crossed paths with the Mayan world, the mountains and jungles, the people, the temples, the birds, the fantastic creation tales and the Popol Vuh.

# Journey

## Lake Atitlan and Tikal

In June 1992, I was quite pleased to find myself on honeymoon in Guatemala. My partner Estrella and I flew to Guatemala City and took a precarious taxi ride over the mountain to Antigua Guatemala, the exquisitely beautiful former colonial seat of the country. We stayed with a friend on a typical shuttered street where tall doors abutted the cobbled roadway and opened onto verdant inner courtyards with spacious quarters. For several days, we absorbed the colorful commotion of the main plaza, shops, Mayans in native dress, and the large compliment of foreign visitors. At dinner one evening, we met a Dutch woman artist who lived in Santiago Atitlan. She invited us to stay with her if we went up that way. So we did.

Lake Atitlan is a large body of water in the Highlands, usually placid except, of course, when thunderstorms sweep across it. The craft that ply its waters for fish and transport would be swamped in a tempest. The lake is nestled in a circle of hills and several volcanoes. The road from Guatemala City deposits you in the hub town of Panahachel, known as Gringotanango because it is a haven for transient North Americans. Directly across the lake from Panahachel and within sight is Santiago Atitlan. But it may take the passenger boat one or two hours to arrive there because it stops at villages along the way as it circumnavigates the lake. There is no serviceable road around the lake. Gringos like us seldom venture far from lakeside villages. The hardy Mayans walk up and over the hills.

The lake is a provider, a creative force. From its depth, its watery womb, a people were born through the vulva like aperture in the cleft between the hills at Santiago Atitlan. They went on to populate the earth and give thanks, burning incense, making offerings, growing corn, painting. All of this is alive and well today as we witnessed in the artists we met, in the Cofradia rituals (living indigenous traditions) in which we participated and

7

in the community celebrations in the village plaza. How animated was this place and its people. Its intoxicating magic already held me.

Then back in Antigua Guatemala for a night, we arranged for a hasty departure the next morning to catch a flight from Guatemala City to Flores to visit the ruins at Tikal. Another hairy ride over the mountain, this time in a van with a dozen patrons, some in folding chairs. The driver did a great job and we made it to the airport in one piece and on time. The flight itself was a short hop.

After settling into our hotel room on the grounds of the state park where Tikal is located, we made a late afternoon foray to the temples. These monuments have been called the "Stonehenge of the West". I knew only what most gringos know: that the builders had a bloody ballgame and the civilization collapsed over a thousand years ago. An easy hike found us in the Great Plaza of Tikal. It was nearly deserted by that hour.

I climbed the steps of a huge temple. Aided by the graciously afforded local magical help of screeching parrots, my vision kicked into gear as I surveyed the Plaza. The scene was stunning. In the middle of hundreds of square miles of jungle, there stood exquisitely crafted stone temples rising above the canopy of lush green. The silence pulsated with a vibrant hum as tropical air rose to fill my nostrils with fragrant scents of vegetation.

I was perched at the top of the Temple of Masks which rose in three massive tiers. It had a roof comb, a small structure with an inner chamber that looked like it functioned as a changing or waiting room. A narrow platform outside the roof comb faced steep steps that dropped to the Plaza floor. Facing me from the opposite end of the Plaza (several hundred meters), the Temple of the Giant Jaguar sat in stoic silence. It rose in nine tiers of immense stone blocks to the same height as its sister temple. It too had a roof comb and platform. It seemed that two people could stand on the roof comb platforms at either end of the Great Plaza and speak in conversational tones with each other as their voices carried above the tree line.

Along the length of the Plaza on the north side were lesser temples and monuments with inscribed stelae, round stone altars, and huge stone faces of the deities. On the south side of the Plaza was a complex of quadrangles that may have been dwellings. I lingered on the Temple top above the Plaza, feeling the power of the stones seep into me. They were gray with traces of stucco white like skeletal bones. The color and flesh were gone. Until relatively recently these stones were covered by centuries of jungle growth. Then came the diggers and scrapers who laid them bare. But these skeletal stones still held an energy that emanated incredible currents.

The jungle and the stones began to put me in trance. What would it be like if the temples were stuccoed white, painted in their reds and yellows to contrast with the jungle greens? What if feathered headdresses came alive under swaying bodies, drumming and singing incantations? An inner tug pulled me to time travel, to know the magic and power as it had been made when Tikal was in full bloom. Then my better magical self snapped me out of it. I clapped three times and said my name aloud. Time travel is not in my repertoire.

The next day we explored the more outlying complexes of Tikal. Until at last, we thanked the ancestors, magical helpers and bid farewell this time. Then we flew back to San Francisco.

In the days that followed our return, I gathered what relevant literature I could find from the bookshelves of my housemates, a guidebook to Central America and an art history volume on Mesoamerica. I learned, among other things, that the Mayan creation myth centered on a sacred ballgame played with a rubber ball of their own invention. Hero Twin Gods squared off against the Lords of the Underworld. In the context of a ballgame, the Hero Twins were sacrificed but came back to life (or did not actually die) and eventually overcame the Lords of the Underworld by magical acts. Photo plates of stone carvings and ceramic figurines of ballplayers depicted scenes of decapitation and vegetal rebirth from bloody corpses. Were losers made bloody victims to ensure that the corn grew, or did the carvings represent symbol only?

I had wondered why a ball court adjoined the Temple of the Giant Jaguar at Tikal. Now the purpose of a ball court in that setting became clear. The epic struggles of the Mayan creation, the cycles of the sun, the moon, the seasons, and birth, death, and rebirth were all played out in a ritual ballgame. It was a fascinating revelation.

Suddenly, while contemplating these weighty questions, I leapt to the present and thought, "Of course, that's why the seasonal games of football, baseball, and basketball that rule the men who rule are so important. Our games are the modern version of the ancient sacred ritual ballgames of the Mayans." It wasn't as though I could see a direct linear connection between the Mayan past and the American present. The connection was energy and purpose. Mayan male rulers, priests, nobility and players of the game believed that their ballgame rituals regulated the flow of the life blood of their world. My fellow American men of the gridiron, diamond, and hardwood do not see themselves as Heroes of an epic creation and celestial struggle. Or do they? Is it deeply buried and denied? Are the games of today an attempt to control the elements of nature just as the ancient games attempted?

Intrigued by the comparison/connection of the modern and ancient games, I investigated further, heading east from San Francisco to the De-. partment of Anthropology, UC Berkeley. The library is a comfortable place to work. If you sit near the large windows, there are hills and real grass to gaze upon while day dreaming. The Mayan collection is a few feet away. And most excellent, the Café Strada across the street is a very satisfactory place to sip a latte and put in the obligatory coffee house session. It was easy to justify $100 for a library card so I could check out books.

Mayan scholarship has grown by leaps and bounds in recent years and continues unabated. Huge strides have been made in deciphering the hieroglyphic writings, enabling translators to accurately describe the Mayan cosmology. Demographic studies of Mayan ruins have shed an increasingly bright light on the ecological and cultural causes for the demise of the classic Mayan centers. But, in my early excursion into the writings about the Maya, I was drawn to one historical person in particular. The arrogant, tragic figure of 18 Rabbit epitomized all that was spectacular and ruinous about the classic Maya.

18 Rabbit ruled the kingdom of Copan (in modern Honduras) from 695 CE until 738 CE, though 18 Rabbit was not his original Mayan name. He came by the 18 Rabbit moniker due to an archeologist's error. Instead of reading the king's name glyph as 18 Images of God, the number 18 was mistakenly combined with an image that looked like a rabbit. The error was eventually discovered but the name 18 Rabbit stuck.

In January 738 CE, the fortieth year of his impressive reign, 18 Rabbit's master carvers and painters put the finishing touches on the final version of the main ball court in Copan, arguably the most splendid ball court in the Mayan world and second in size only to the great ball court at Chichen Itza in the Yucatan.

After the ball court was completed, 18 Rabbit most likely joined a war party intent on bringing back captives from Quirigua, a fiefdom within the orbit of Copan about thirty miles northeast. Presumably, the intended captives were slated to play an unhappy role in sacrificial rituals at the new ball court and at the same time, the war party might quell a possible rebellion in the making. Instead, 18 Rabbit himself was captured, then ritually sacrificed on 3 May 738 CE at the hands of Kawak-Sky, lord of Quirigua, and perhaps a relative of 18 Rabbit.

These historic facts were deciphered from the hieroglyphic writings at Quirigua and Copan. But the scraps of story available to us hardly begin to convey the universe shattering impact of 18 Rabbit's defeat and death. The entire cosmos of the Mayan world at Copan was linked to the divine god king. He was the living thread connecting the movement of the constellations, the sun and moon, the morning and evening star. He was the embodiment of the world tree, holding together sky, earth, underworld. He stood in the place of the Hero Twins to play ball against the Lords of the Underworld. It was unthinkable that the warrior god king could be defeated.

But he was defeated. And 18 Rabbit's sad tale might be seen to presage the demise of the classic Mayan kingship system. Within two hundred years of 18 Rabbit's fall, the overall "collapse" occurred and a thick blanket of jungle growth had claimed the crumbling ancient temples.

I realized that my next trip to the Maya heartland had to be to Copan Ruinas (the village and complex of monuments). I had to check out 18 Rabbit's incomparable ball court for myself. Would I be able to sense any of the ballgame action, considering I'd arrive 1200 years after the fact? Possessing a ballgame pilgrim's optimistic premonition, something told me that the stones still spoke.

# Copan

Spanning parts of the 7th and 8th centuries CE, the reign of 18 Rabbit coincided with the most intensive construction of ceremonial monuments in the Mayan world. And 18 Rabbit was foremost among them. Besides the ball court, Copan's artists completed stunning works upon standing stones, often depicting their ruler. The Mayanist scholar, William L. Fash, said, "18 Rabbit was the greatest single patron of the arts in Copan's history, based on the number of his works and on the contribution of an extremely naturalistic, fluid, high-relief style of carving." This intense period of monument building also coincided with an increase in warfare between Mayan city-states.

The end-game of Classic Mayan civilization came in the early 10th century when Copan, along with most of the Mayan centers, was abandoned to the jungle. Evidence later indicated that termination rituals were performed. That is, monuments appear to have been purposely defaced so as to indicate that this way of life was over.

Then, after nine centuries under tropical growth, Copan was "discovered" in the Western anglo sense by John Stephens and Frederick Catherwood. Stephens was an American lawyer who preferred to travel (ostensibly for health reasons). He secured a roving ambassadorial post to further his real passion. Catherwood was an illustrator from England. They had earlier collaborated on Egyptian travels before setting out in 1839 for their Central American adventure. Stephens' popular travel narrative and Catherwood's brilliant drawings are as fresh today as when they published their work in 1841.

Stephens wrote that after grueling travel by mule, they reached the ruins of Copan. Their machete wielding guide (one of the few locals who was familiar with the site) cleared a path through the dense foliage. Large processions of monkeys raced through the tree canopy, screeching as they went as if to berate the intruders for disturbing the sleep of the city the monkeys had been left to guard. Sitting upon a temple and contemplating the wonders he glimpsed for the first time, Stephens noted:

> "…architecture, sculpture, and painting, all the arts which embellish life, had flourished in this overgrown forest; orators, warriors, and statesmen, beauty, ambition, and glory, had lived and passed away, and none knew that such things had been, or could tell of their past existence … The city was desolate … It lay before us like a shattered bark in the midst of the ocean, her masts gone, her name effaced, her crew perished, and none to tell whence she came, to whom she belonged, how long on her voyage, or what caused her destruction .. All was mystery, dark, impenetrable mystery, and every circumstance increased it. In Egypt the colossal skeletons of gigantic temples stand in unwa- tered sands in all the nakedness of desolation; here an immense forest shrouded the ruins, hiding them from sight, heightening the impression and moral effect, and giving an intensity and almost wildness to the interest."

In the nearly two centuries since Stephens' evocative impression of Copan, the ruins have generated a steady current of interest. Copan is one of the most studied sites in the Mayan world. These days, the Honduran government directs the excavations and study projects. A spanking new museum has been built at the site.

I would go to Copan in my dual capacity as ballplayer and Witch.

Ballplaying is at the core of my being. I do not have a memory of when I wasn't a ballplayer. The ball (any ball) is comfortable in my hands — its touch, feel, weight. Even at age seven or eight, the big-kid quarterback in playground touch football games threw to me because my "good hands" reliably caught the ball. In later years, I developed a deadly jump shot on the basketball court that saw me through high school and college teams. A feeling for the movement of ballplayers and the flight of the ball is second nature. This trip to Copan would be like a visit to any other ballpark — check out the field, soak in the atmosphere, get a feeling for the players and the game. Are they any good? Did I want to stay and watch?

As a practitioner of eco-feminist Witchcraft, I have facilitated community rituals celebrating the lunar, solar and seasonal cycles. In the U.S. and Europe, I have co-led workshops using trance, dance, storytelling, and music in rituals to explore the personal transformative possibilities within myths and folktales ranging from the Inanna cycle of Mesopotamia to the

Slavic Baba Yaga. The caves, rivers, and stone circles of Europe have given me wonderful occasion for sacred ritual. In Copan, I would peer beneath the ball court, the ballplayers and the ballgame to the underlying meaning of the ritual, putting to use my experience as a ritual creator to assess how the Mayan ballgame moved energy and toward what end.

# Copan Ruinas

In January 1993, I returned to Guatemala City, rented a car, and set out for Copan with Estrella. She was my ace in the hole. It is always useful, when playing ball or practicing magic in unfamiliar terrain, to bring along a ringer — someone you can throw into the fray with confidence at a critical point. I didn't feel that I needed her help with the ballgame but was sure that her talents would be very welcome in sensing the energy and ritual practice on a larger scale. Knowing that she was on the bench, ready to come in, made me feel well prepared for the game as we winged our way south.

Employing my former cabdriver savvy in negotiating our way out of Guatemala City, we drove east on Route 9, a two lane road that hugs a mountain ridge parallel to the Rio Montagua (on its path from the highlands to the Gulf of Honduras). The winding high road eventually gave way to the lowlands with their immense fruit plantations. Four hours of hot, tedious driving (trailing exhaust spewing trucks and buses on the upgrades) brought us to Rio Hondo in the heart of fruit country. From here Route 10 took us past the towns of Zacapa and Chiquimula. At the turn-off for Route 11, the paved road became a dirt road that for the next fifty kilometers threw up a cloud of fine dust in the wake of every vehicle.

Ten hours into our drive, we came to the village of El Florido where we went through the process of completing several forms at modest wooden structures on both sides of the border, paying ten Quetzales/Limpuras for every stamp of a form. The image of this transaction that stays with me is of a wall inside the Honduran border control building. Bundles of processed forms like the ones we just finished were stacked floor to ceiling next to the wall. The progression of aged, yellowing paper over the expanse of the wall, as the bundles went from the deep yellow of the 1940s to the white of the 1990s, struck me as an odd bureaucratic art piece.

A stream crossed the road twenty yards from the border control buildings. I hoped that it was not too deep for our small rental car. But that was the least of it. The ex-pat American car rental agent in Guatemala City cautioned us that the road from the border to Copan was rough. We did make it to Copan alright but it was harrowing. It took me two hours to drive twelve kilometers, avoiding the chasms (ruts) so as not to seriously damage the underbelly of the car. We passed a VW bus of Germans who were not as lucky. The Honduran government's apparent strategy in leaving the road in such condition was to encourage tourists to fly to the Honduran town of San Pedro Sula, spend some cash there, and take the paved road from San Pedro Sula to Copan.

It was a pleasant evening when we finally reached the dimly lit village square of Copan. For one Honduran Limpura, a boy guided us to a hotel that we easily could have found ourselves. After the ubiquitous chicken dinner at a restaurant across from the hotel, we strolled around the square, watching village kids kicking a ball while the tinny sound of spirituals from an evangelical church filtered into the night air. We slept well in the humid tropical air, looking forward to our exploration of the temples.

In the morning, we lingered over pancakes, making a late start for the ruins. I was excited. It felt like game day. I was not in a hurry, though, because there was no kick-off time. We walked the cobblestone streets of the busy village and over a bridge where women washed clothes in a stream. The hot, noon sun glared from the green leaves of corn rows in the fields as country and tourist life commingled along the one kilometer from town to ruins. Three air-conditioned buses sat in the corner of a spacious parking lot adjacent to a modern administration center. Children hovered close by, trying to sell cheap replicas of the stelae. We bought tickets and entered the grounds of the ruins which gave the impression of a well kept national park. Not a speck of litter could be found. A wide shaded walkway (one of the original causeways built by the Mayans) led to the entrance gate of the principal group of monuments. This was it. The moment was at hand. I could see beyond the tree line that a still expanse of grass opened to reveal the silent, stately, stones. Smiling inwardly, I stepped from the shade of the path into the sun drenched energetic field of the majestic yet greatly muted monuments.

Entering from the west, I quickly found my bearings without the aid of a guide or guidebook because I had spent many hours before this trip pouring over photos and maps of the ruins.

Straight ahead, in the center of the Great Plaza, was the "navel of the world", a monument of comparatively small size but of large significance. It rose in four squared tiers to a platform about forty feet from the Plaza floor. On each of its four sides, there were steps to the top. It looked like a stone wedding cake. This monument very probably represented the "umbilical cord" of the Mayan creation myth from which the cosmic "modelers, makers" created the "four fold siding, the four corners" of the Mayan world (the universal house) in the middle of the sea/earth plain (the Great Plaza).

To the north of the four directions monument stretched the Great Plaza, dotted with standing stone stelae depicting 18 Rabbit, for the most part, with zoomorphic altars at the feet of the stelae. Enclosed on three sides by steps that seemed to form an amphitheater, the Great Plaza might hold thousands on important ritual occasions. South of the four directions monument were the main ball court, the Hieroglyphic Stairway (commissioned by 18 Rabbit), and the imposing man made stone mountains (temples) of the "Acropolis" that rose high above the floor of the Plaza. Deep in these temples lay the bones of the founders of Copan.

My companion wandered off to explore the Great Plaza while I made a bee-line for the ball court. I took a seat on the steps at the north "end zone" of the "I" shaped ball court. This end of the court was enclosed. The south end of the court was open, giving an unimpeded sightline to those seated anywhere on the Acropolis, a little distance from the court. The playing surface of the ball court was about eight meters wide and forty meters long, encompassed on each side by sloping walls without steps.

As I began to relax, a knowing half smile replaced the inner smile of excitement and anticipation. It was so familiar. After fifteen minutes, I could not get over how "at home" I felt at this ball court. It had an energy that I knew very, very well. The reverie conjured by the stones brought me back to my youth and the grass gridiron at Syracuse University where I used to sneak into the football games. It seemed I was sneaking in again. Faded memories of football players warming up before a college game blended with impressions of Mayan ballplayers warming up in the end zone in front of me.

"Yeah, this is it," I nodded to myself. The Mayan players joked around and showed off their skills, belying a game that would be in deadly earnest when the ritual began. These guys were incredibly good, definitely major league. Their control and passing of the hard black rubber ball with hips, chest, thighs and forearms was as precise as any ball playing I have ever seen. I sat for twenty minutes more, taking in as much as I could, entranced by the sloping walls and the macaw heads that faced off against one another from opposite sides of the court.

Then my concentration started to flag and I had to move, having sensed as much as I could in that spot. Small groups of tourists passed, loudly talking as they climbed the ball court. Their sightseeing energy was not conducive to plumbing the depths of the magic of the stones. Anyway, I was a tourist myself and had no special permission of a magical nature to do more than sit. I did, however, ask Grandmother's permission to be present in the general sense, that is, to be there and see what I could see but without leave to engage in my own ritual in that space. Grandmother is the true authority in the Mayan world. But, that's redundant since Grandmother is the true authority everywhere, in all her guises. Wherever you go, if you come with clean hands, Grandmother will always give you permission to see what you can see. Of course, she may first ask to see your hands.

Following the lead of my fellow tourists, I climbed the rear of the ball court and ambled the narrow reviewing area running the length of each side of the ball court's sloping walls. Despite the advanced aging process of hundreds of years in the tropics, the macaw heads were striking and frightening in their beauty. Standing in the middle of the court, looking down the slope where the center marker would have been, I saw how the game (ritual) may have begun. The rubber ball could have been "dropped" into the center from the height of the top of the slope, much like a jump ball in basketball. I was pleased at having sensed this possibility concerning a point that had perplexed me.

On our second day at Copan, we meandered by the banks of the Rio Copan amid quiet corn fields and shaded cow paths, out of sight and sound of other tourists. In a wooded clearing on the path to the river, there was an earlier version of a ball court, about a fourth the size of the main ball court. I tossed a small, blue, hard rubber handball in the air and against the walls of this deserted ball court of creation.

In the afternoon, we hung out under the trees next to the Great Plaza, watching successive knots of tourists being taken through their paces. At the end of the day, we compared notes about our impressions thus far.

I was mildly surprised that we converged on our sense of the directional flow of the ritual energy at Copan. The East Court of the Acropolis may have been the starting point of a progression of rituals lasting several days. A minor or "false" ball court (three court markers only) lies in the East Court. And in a corner of the East Court, there may be the "Bat House", the scene of a critically important stage in the reenactment of the Hero Twins' underworld journey to death and back. The dimensions of the East Court suggested that there was a more exclusive set of ritual participants in this setting.

The ritual sequence may have begun in the East Court, place of the rising sun, with an elite group, moved west to the main Acropolis, then north to the ball court. More people witnessed the ballgame than the rituals in and about the Acropolis but the size and enclosed nature of the ball court seems to indicate that the ballgame did not play before the largest gathering. Rather, the Great Plaza most likely was where the crowds witnessed the thrilling climax. The guides' blanket assertions to the tourists that "... the captives were sacrificed on the altars at the feet of the standing stone stelae ..." (in the Great Plaza) made energetic and ritual sense.

The god-king and royal shamans could draw on the power of the ancestors buried in the depths of the Acropolis to form a huge ball or wave of energy that gained in steam as it moved through the ritualized ballgames and on to the Great Plaza where thousands waited impatiently for the communal frenzy of the blood sacrifice. It was a hot ritual. That much is certain.

After this part of our chat, Estrella remarked that she was struck by the fact that she felt no female energy at Copan. Coming here assuming that there would be elements of a nature religion, she found the regenerative energy and touch of women simply absent. I was jarred by her comment because I immediately saw it to be true. I was so in tune with the male ball playing energy at Copan that I overlooked the absence of female energy until she pointed it out. Female and natural symbols of birth, death, and rebirth were present but the cut of the stones and the energy in the monuments spoke of the containment of women and nature within a competitive, violent, bloody male ritual.

The legacy of the mighty ballplayer/king, 18 Rabbit, was conspicuously present in Copan. His portraits carved in stone in the Great Plaza were exquisite to behold. Yet, the arrogance that even now continues to infuse his effigies is palpable to the touch. Never, I think, has the lofty hero fallen low been more dramatically personified. From the height of the Mayan creation myth in the starry constellations, 18 Rabbit fell to unredeemed death in the bowels of the underworld. There would be no bouncing back like the Hero Twins. He was captured, had his beating heart cut from his chest, was tied up in the shape of a ball, and rolled down stone steps (a very possible scenario).

It is an image that befits the soul of Copan. There is magnificent art but no heart. There is a gaping hole where the heart should be.

Sudden, complete, devastating, 18 Rabbit's fall probably struck speechless every segment of Copan's society. Even rebellious nobles, who may have muttered "Down with 18 Rabbit", must have been as dumbfounded as his supporters. The whole of Copan had been organized around the construction and maintenance of the ritual complex — from the cutting, moving, and placing of stone over centuries, to clearing forests to make fires to produce lime stucco for monument decoration, to growing the corn, beans, and squash to feed the elite class of ritualists. At last the grand illusion was unmasked.

The humiliating defeat of 18 Rabbit sent Copan into a deep funk. Their territorial integrity was not abridged because, for the most part, the kind of warfare that led to land conquest was not prevalent. But, speaking of the aftermath of 18 Rabbit's debacle, William Fash offered the understatement, "Copan entered a period of dormancy."

Twenty years post 18 Rabbit, the 15th ruler in the Copan dynasty, Smoke Shell, tried to offer a more favorable interpretation of the unfortunate events. Inscriptions that Smoke Shell commissioned for the Hieroglyphic Stairway emphasized the heroic warrior exploits of Smoke Imix God K and other predecessors of 18 Rabbit, whose defeat was lightly skipped over. A decoder of the Hieroglyphic Stairway said that the inscriptions by Smoke Shell had the feeling of a revivalist movement about them.

The last stone monument to be erected in Copan was in 822 CE. Called Altar L, it marked the accession of a pretender named U Cit Tok to the throne. The impending collapse was near and Altar L was never finished, left uncarved on one side. U Cit Tok had attempted to unify Copan by founding a new dynasty. He, however, was the dynasty's first and last member. As the central authority of kingship declined with the unsuccessful attempt of U Cit Tok to unify Copan, a demoralized people drifted away from the kingdom of stone. The urban and rural populations of Copan, in the final stages of kingship, suffered increased disease and malnutrition. The Copan valley lost half its population from 850 CE to 925 CE.

Deforestation was the single greatest underlying cause of the demise of Copan. The ruling elite were obsessed with their roles in Copan's society. The building of monuments, decorating and redecorating them in a show of status, drove the ecology of Copan beyond the breaking point. Huge quantities of wood were required for fires hot enough to make lime stucco for the surfaces of the palaces and monuments. The forests of the Copan valley were hacked down. The resulting erosion filled the peat swamps where moss was collected to fertilize the fields and terraced gardens. In time, neither the royal class nor the common class could be fed from the denuded and increasingly unproductive land.

After three days at Copan, we toured the site once more and gave our thanks to the ancestors and spirits who let us see what we could see. It seemed to me that I was leaving behind a reservoir of unredeemed and unhappy human spirituality in Copan.

The ballplayers were there, just below the surface, stuck in a ritual that begged to be transformed. I could feel them, waiting and watching in the underworld — ever hopeful.

# Quirigua

The other piece of the puzzle in the story of 18 Rabbit lies about thirty miles from Copan in Guatemala, on the banks of the Rio Montagua, at Quirigua.

Retracing our journey over the rutted road back to the border crossing at El Florido, we made it as far as Rio Hondo on Route 9 and stayed the night. The following day I was tempted to forego Quirigua and carry on to Guatemala City and Antigua Guatemala thinking that I had seen what I needed to see.

A jaunt to Quirigua would take us a half day in the opposite direction. Thankfully Estrella egged us on to Quirigua. The experience gave me an insight into precisely the flip side of the ballgame equation I witnessed in Copan.

Quirigua was an hour and a half from our motel, heading east toward the sea. In classic Mayan times, Quirigua was a stop on a well traveled trade route. The Rio Montagua was a lifeline, a largely navigable river from the base of the highlands in Guatemala to the Gulf of Honduras. At the turn-off from Route 9 to Quirigua, a well maintained dirt road led past vast banana plantations to the site of the ruins.

No one happened to be at the entrance to take our fee, so we walked onto the grounds of lush green grass. The air was heavier at Quirigua than at the higher river valley of Copan. Even the jungle seemed thicker. The core monumental site was much smaller than at Copan, maybe only twenty percent as large as the latter. At the end of a long narrow grassy patch with standing stone stelae and zoomorphic altars, a group of temples circled the main plaza. I could not for the life of me locate the ball court until I consulted a detailed map. The ball court was unexcavated and amounted to two barely visible parallel mounds close to the central temples. The comparison between the ball court at Copan and the mere outline of a ball court at Quirigua could not be more telling. It was the difference between a gem of the Mayan classic period and a humble edifice in a river town.

At Quirigua, though, the tables were turned in a most unimaginable way. Hoping to quell an unruly vassal, stamp out conspiracies, and secure tribute goods, 18 Rabbit apparently led a war party to Quirigua. But his gods failed him. Almost certainly, he was ambushed and captured along the way. What I felt in the ruins was the faded energy of an awestruck assembly who witnessed an unbelievable upset. There was the residue of an almost uncontrollable light headed giddiness at the sight of 18 Rabbit's colossal defeat on their home court. Standing in the center of the main plaza, Estrella casually remarked that 18 Rabbit was probably rolled down the steps we were facing. Whether by power of suggestion or the past showing itself, I saw the image of the fallen king tied in a ball and bouncing down the stone steps of the Acropolis at Quirigua.

Quirigua sometimes gets short shrift in relation to Copan although it's Stela C importantly references the Mayan 4th Creation date. However, Quirigua does surpass Copan in one notable respect. Quirigua has the tallest stone stelae in all of Mesoamerica. After the defeat of 18 Rabbit, the lord of Quirigua, Kawak-Sky, erected several stone stelae in his image that are over twice the height of the stelae of 18 Rabbit at Copan. It was a definite statement. Kawak-Sky had the biggest one.

\* \* \* \* \* \*

Back home in San Francisco once again, I knew that I gained what I sought in Copan — a feel for the game, the land, the fallen king. 18 Rabbit's ball court confirmed early suspicions and presented new ones. Now I could articulate what every ballplayer knows in their bones, that the ballgame has a higher purpose. But I could not articulate it fully. I needed to know more if I wanted to have a handle on what made 18 Rabbit and the ballgame tick.

A close reading of the Popol Vuh ushered in the dawning, the light.

# Popol Vuh

*"Popol Vuh is one of the great books about the creation of the world.
It is the Mayan Bible."*
— Carlos Fuentes

*"Popol Vuh … is, beyond any shadow of doubt,
the most distinguished example of native American
literature that survived the passing centuries."*
— Sylvanus G. Morley

From the middle of the 19th century, when the Popol Vuh was brought to world attention by a Spanish translation published in Austria and a French translation published in Paris, and continuing to the present era, the Popol Vuh has been seen in the light described above by the author, Fuentes, and the scholar, Morley. The passage of time, coupled with breakthroughs in deciphering Mayan hieroglyphs, has only served to strengthen this favorable view of the Popol Vuh's authenticity, antiquity, and commonality among Mayans as their creation story through the ages.

The Popol Vuh (Book of the Mat, Book of Community, Book of Counsel) was compiled by one or more native authors of the K'iche Maya in highland Guatemala in the mid-16th century (probably 1554 to 1558 CE). Writing their oral history from memory and perhaps with the aid of a few hieroglyphic works, the indigenous authors used Latin script taught them by missionaries to compose their K'iche language.

The Popol Vuh is a prime example of a "charter myth", i.e., a quasi-historical myth that explains the creation and history of a people while conferring ruling authority on a specific hereditary line. The story begins in the great void, goes through several phases of creation, and concludes with the living descendants of the K'iche Maya, who are comprised of clans headed by a male "mother-father". In some degree, the particular spin the Popol

Vuh takes may be colored by political conflict within the K'iche"nation" at the time of writing.

And although the Popol Vuh originates in a remote highland town in the 16th century, it substantially mirrors classic Mayan mythology from a thousand years earlier, encompassing stories from mountain highlands, jungle lowlands and the Yucatan Peninsula. In covering thousands of square miles and hundreds of years, the universality of the story in the Popol Vuh is truly remarkable.

# Text

The original 16th century manuscript of the Popol Vuh by the K'iche authors was lost. However, Friar Francisco Ximenez, parish priest of Santo Tomas Chichicastenango in the K'iche highlands from 1701 to 1703, obtained a "copy" of the "original" manuscript from a Mayan parishioner. A prodigious historian and linguist, Friar Ximenez had an excellent grasp of the K'iche Mayan dialect. Of the Popol Vuh, he wrote,"...I found that it was the doctrine which they first imbided with their mother's milk, and that all of them knew it almost by heart ..." (AR)

Friar Ximenez copied the K'iche copy and made a Spanish translation. He aligned the K'iche text with the Spanish text in parallel rows on each page. This K'iche/Spanish manuscript was kept in the Dominican convent in Chichicastenango until 1829 when the religious houses (convents, monasteries) in Guatemala were closed and their archives sent to the University Library in Guatemala City.

An Austrian, Carl Scherzer, came across the Ximenez K'iche/Spanish manuscript at the library in Guatemala City in 1853 and published Ximenez' Spanish version in Vienna in 1856. Also, a French cleric, Abbe Charles Etienne Brasseur de Bourbourg, viewed the Ximenez K'iche/Spanish manuscript in 1855. However, Brasseur de Bourbourg did not content himself with looking. He "borrowed" the manuscript and spirited it to Paris. There, he published his French translation in 1861. Eventually, a copy of the Ximenez K'iche/Spanish manuscript found its way into the antiquities collection in Europe of Edward E. Ayers. In 1911, the manuscript passed with much of Ayer's collection to the Newberry Library in Chicago. There it rests.

The Popol Vuh has been translated into Spanish, French, German, English, Italian, Japanese, Russian. There are five English translations. Lewis Spence's 1908 translation had the advantage of being first. It had the disadvantage of being an incomplete summary written for a popular mythology series. Adrian Recinos' 1947 Spanish translation (English version by Goetz and Morley 1950) was complete, scholarly and written by a native Guatemalan. Recinos was the person most responsible for ferreting out the history of the Popol Vuh manuscript. Munro Edmonson's 1971 translation attempted a style change from the prose of previous translations to the poetic form of the original K'iche. Dennis Tedlock's 1985 (rev. 1996) translation benefited greatly from the dramatic advances in Mayan studies during intervening years. Allen Christenson added a further translation in 2003. Tedlock's is still the standard work.

Interestingly, the consistency of the story line among all the translations is very strong. Munro Edmonson's comment still holds. "After all the versions are compared, it is notable that the discrepancies are startingly minor."

# Rationale

There are three reasons for the existence of the Popol Vuh.

The most pressing reason is stated by the Mayan authors in the opening paragraph. The anonymous writers acknowledge that they are living in a Christian society. And the "word" that is the K'iche story can no longer be seen. It is hidden, lost. There is no longer a "book" (hieroglyphic document) to consult. In fact, the authors are too polite or politic to say that their sacred books were burned by the conquering Spanish. The first reason, then, is to set down and preserve the essence of their tradition.

The second reason for the existence of the Popol Vuh is internal to the story and relates to lost eyesight. Halfway through the Popol Vuh the first four humans are at last created. They were handsome "men". They could see everything in heaven and on earth perfectly. This alarmed the Gods. The Gods decided to limit the sight of humans so that only a portion could be seen. Hurakan (Heart of Sky) breathed a cloud over the eyes of the first humans. But the lords of K'iche had a remedy for this clouded vision. They had a book which restored this lost eyesight. With this book, they could see to the four corners of space and time, to see past, present and future. It was Popol Vuh (Council Book).

A third reason for the existence of the Popol Vuh is also internal to the story but it hinges on the nature of the myth. The purpose of the Popol Vuh, in its oral and written forms, is to justify and memorialize the rule of heaven and earth by men, to sanction with divine authority the sacrificial ballgame warrior way of life. The Popol Vuh is a creation story that moves a basically egalitarian village culture toward a more hierarchical, war-like society.Before humans are made, the story will show that the Maize God usurps the blood magic, the creative birthing powers of Blood Moon in order to establish a new line. The Maize God already has twin sons, One Monkey and One Artisan, who are flautists, carvers, singers, gardeners. But, the Maize God impregnates Blood Moon in the underworld and she gives birth to the Hero Twins, the ballgame warriors, who play ball with her symbolic heart (the rubber "blood ball"). The Maize God's first set of twin sons are brushed aside and sent back to the forest by their younger brothers, the ballgame warriors. Culturally, politically, and sexually, the singing garden boys were replaced by the ballgame warrior boys. When humans arrive, they will follow the lead of the Gods. Grandmother Time will be enlisted to frame the story within her count of days.

# My Standing

Of course, no one owns the Popol Vuh save the K'iche community from whence it came.

I have no standing to tell the story that is the Popol Vuh or to interpret its content. I come to the Popol Vuh as a petitioner. I come as a ballplayer asking permission of Grandmother to look at the game her boys play. I promise no trickery or ridicule. I've also asked Maximon in Santiago Atitlan for his blessing in my writing. I hope that my version of events and running commentary does not offend.

I encourage the reader to consider the full texts of the Popol Vuh that I have noted and draw on rather than simply the idiosyncratic highlights that appeal to me. Far better still to travel to Mayan lands to touch the stones and be with those who carry the old traditions into the present. It should be said, though, that you could be changed forever. When an unsuspecting art historian, (the late) Linda Schele, visited Palenque in the Mayan lowlands on a family holiday, she became irretrievably entranced. Twenty years and several books later, Ms. Schele had become a noted expert on Mayan hieroglyphs and cosmology. You may not become a scholar like Linda Schele or a ballplayer hoping for a wee kick a'boot with the Hero Twins like me, but if you go, you'll be bitten.

I begin the game with the advantage and the baggage of being a Polish/Irish/Lithuanian American, pacifist/anarchist, eco-feminist, ball playing, honky tonk Witch. No doubt there are other starting points — the pure scholar alleging no bias, the seer tuning in the galactic mind in Mayan myth, the Numerologist counting with the Mayans. I find that even where I disagree with some or most of a particular viewpoint, there is always something useful in the variety of approaches taken toward the Mayan tales. I must leave the intricate details of Mayan calendrics to the scholars. Nor will I critique others' conclusions at length. Putting across my own interpretation is my goal. But I do find it helpful to disclose built in biases rather than deny their existence.

Now that I have made my biases painfully clear, I can say, as the Lords of Death will say to the Hero Twins, "Okay, let's go play ball!", and proceed to the Root of the K'iche Word.

# Root of the K'iche Word

The authors of the Popol Vuh commence their narration of the mysteries, the root of the K'iche by naming the divine ones who are responsible for all that is:

**Tzacol, Bitol:** Creator and Maker, Former and Shaper, Maker and Modeler.

**Alom, Qaholom:** Mother and Father, Bearer and Engenderer, Bearer and Begetter.

**Hun-Ahpu Vuch:** Possum and Coyote.

**Hun-Ahpu Utiu:** Dawn and Night.

**Zaqui-Nima-Tziis:** Great White Peccary, Coati, Mother of God.

**Tepeu:** Majesty Quetzal Serpent,Quq-cumatz Sovereign Plumed Serpent, Serpent covered with green feathers.

**U Qux Cho:** Heart of Lake,U Qux Palo Heart of Sea.

**Ah Raxa Laq:** Green plate shaper.

**Ah Raxa Tzel:** Blue bowl shaper.

**Iyom, Mamon:** Grandmother and Grandfather, Mid-wife and Matchmaker.

**Xpiyacoc, Xmucane:** Old man and Old woman.

It was these beings who said everything, did everything, knew everything. Since the time of Christianity, though, the book that revealed these wonders, that told of the dawning was hidden from the reader, the searcher, the thinker.

But the authors continue and say that great was the account of how the sky-earth was formed; how the four sides, the four corners were marked; how the cord was stretched across the sky and over the earth. This was done by the Former and Shaper, the Mother and Father of life, of humans. Here it is, "...the account, the first narrative." (AR)

In the beginning, there was complete stillness. Nothing moved. There was only the sky and the lake/sea. There was not even a ripple in the darkness over the waters. But, those called Mother and Father, Maker and Modeler, Feathered Serpent were in the water. They were encased in blue-green light, covered in quetzel feathers. In the sky was the god, Huracan (Heart of Heaven, Heart of Sky). He had three aspects: Thunder, Lightning, Flash.

Huracan came down from the sky and met with Quetzel Serpent in the waters. These two talked and pondered. They conceived the idea of the birth of humans, who would nourish the gods. They thought more. And when they agreed, they spoke the word "earth". Immediately, mountains rose from the waters. There were valleys and forests. The sky and waters were separated when the earth plain appeared.

## Comment

The beauty, diversity and richness of the images in the Mayan pantheon spring to life in the highlands when a rainstorm descends from the mountain to whip across a lake, or in the dense leafy "green plate" lowland jungle with macaws, quetzals, howler monkeys, and the possibility of an elusive jaguar.

What strikes me about the Mayan pantheon is that the deities appear to be an extension of Grandmother and Grandfather in their many guises. The Maker (cooker) and the Shaper (pottery molder) are "named" Alom (Grandmother, Bearer) and Qaholom (Grandfather, Begetter). She who bears the son and He who begets the son. In animal form, Grandmother and Grandfather are also "called" Possom and Coyote, Great White Peccary and Coati. In natural form, they may be Heart of Heaven and Heart of Earth, Heart of Lake and Heart of Sea. Grandmother and Grandfather are an androgynous, hermaphroditic creative force that permeates life before it ever began.

Yet, even in the opening paragraphs, there is a shift in the making. The overarching primacy of the female/male life force leans in the direction of maleness. Huracan is called a God. Quetzel Serpent is implied to be male. It will not be long in the story before the mother/father of life becomes decidedly male.

In the four sides, four corners, we see the "centering of the world" with the four corner posts (cardinal directions) of the universal house of creation. Later, the Maize God will be raised as the center post of the universal house. Centering the world was the first act of creation and is the first act in any important Mayan enterprise such as dedicating a new field for planting. In ritual terms, centering the world created, defined and sanctified the space in question, whether that space was the world, a gathering in the woods, or a home.

# Three Creations

Heart of Heaven and Feathered Serpent were pleased with their work and thought further. They concluded it would be good for the forests to have guardians. With their thought, they created deer and birds and all the animals. They gave them places to sleep and food to eat. "They gave it, the Mother and Father."

Then the Creator and Modeler instructed the animals to name them, praise them, worship them for they were their mother and father. The animals could not be understood. They just screeched and rattled. Because the animals could not talk and adore their Maker, they were made to accept their fate, they were sacrificed, they were condemned on earth to be killed and eaten.

The Former and Shaper decided to try a second time. Because, as they said, the dawning was close at hand. For this reason, they needed to make a nourisher, a worshiper who would remember them on earth.

A second attempt was made with earth and mud. A body was formed. But it did not look good. It was soggy, crumbling, dissolving. It's face fell to one side. It could not see straight. So, the second work was destroyed and abandoned by the Makers.

The Maker and Modeler conferred once more. This time they resolved to call upon Xpiyacoc and Xmuncane who were far-seers, mid-most seers, soothsayers, diviners, also named Grandmother of Day, Grandmother of Light.

Huracan and Quetzel Serpent implored Xpiyacoc and Xmuncane to divine with corn kernels and incense as to whether wood should be used in a third attempt at creating the human work, at finding a nourisher and sustainer. Grandfather and Grandmother cast lots and affirmed that it would be good to gather and carve the wood. Right away, the manikins were made. They looked and spoke like humans. They had many children and peopled the face of the earth. These woodcarvings were the first numerous people.

But it turned out poorly because the manikins had no heart and no mind. They could not remember the Heart of Heaven. Their bodies were ill-formed. They were dry. They lacked blood, sweat and fat. They wandered around on all fours.

Then the woodcarvings were destroyed. Huracan made a great flood and drowned them. Beasts gouged their eyeballs, tore their flesh, and cut off their heads. The household utensils and animals jeered at them. The dogs and hens said, "Very badly have you treated us, and you have bitten us. Now we bite you in turn." And the cups and dishes said, "Pain and misery you gave us, smoking our tops and sides, cooking us over the fire, burning and hurting us as if we had no feeling. Now it is your turn and you shall burn." (LS)

The manikins ran about wildly trying to escape. They could not hide, either on the rooftops or in the trees or in the caves. Thus, this race, this experiment was ended. It is said, though, that the monkeys who live in the forest are the remainder. Monkeys look like people because they are a sign of a previous attempt at the human work.

## Comment

The motivation of those who are deemed Gods, Huracan and Quetzel Serpent, is extremely intriguing. Since the time of the first sunrise and the first planting is nearing, the Gods need humans to name them, to burn incense, to nurture them. It seems the very purpose of human existence will be to praise the Gods. Definitely, a plan is afoot for the creation of an elite group of ritualists. When, later in the story, the first humans are made, the dawning can take place because the Gods will be praised. And if the consequences visited upon the previous failed creations are any guide, it well behooves the fourth creation (humans) to make the proper offerings and keep the days.

Shifting notions of the curious term mother/father of life continue through the three creations. Huracan and Feathered Serpent call on Xpiyacoc and Xmucane who are those old ones by another name and function. Grandfather, Xpiyacoc, is named first but the "X" prefix means the feminine or small. They both are called Grandmother of Day, Grandmother of Light. Tedlock's translation indicates that Grandmother is "... the day keeper, diviner who stands behind others: Xmucane is her name." (DT)

Is this an admission within the story that Grandmother comes first because she stands behind all others, because she knows and keeps time? Whether an admission or not, in the village cultures that pre-dated the classic Mayan cultures, omnipresent female figurines show that the earth mother as creatrix represented the beliefs and worldview of the earliest Mesoamericans, just as they did for the earliest peoples of Europe. And when the human experiment finally succeeds, it is Grandmother who has moulded "mankind" from ground corn and water. Then, as Grandmother Time, she sets in motion the Mayan Calendar of days according to the natural rhythms of life.

# Seven Times the Color of Fire

At this point, the Popol Vuh veers from the chronological to deal with an apparent emergency. People were not created and the sun had not risen nor were the Hero Twins conceived. Nevertheless, there was a personage who claimed that his "...existence rendered unnecessary that of the sun and moon ..." (LS)

Vucub-Kaqix (Seven Macaw, Seven Parrot, Seven Times the Color of Fire) said that his brilliance would light the way for the formed people, the humans. His eyes were silver, his teeth were emeralds, his nose shone like the moon, the earth became light wherever he passed, so he said. But Vucub-Kaqix only boasted. He magnified himself. His brilliance was not that great. He could not shine or see as far as he said. He was bright only because the sun and moon had not appeared.

It happened that Vucub-Kaqix had two sons, Zipacna and Cabracan (Alligator and Earthquake). These two were arrogant and boastful like their father. Zipacna claimed to be a maker of mountains while Cabracan claimed to destroy mountains.

Hun-Ahpu and Xbalanque (Hero Twins) were not yet born. Still they were Gods and they were angered by the arrogance of Seven Macaw and his sons. The Hero Twins saw great harm in the self-magnification of Seven Macaw before the Heart of Heaven. So the "boys" decided to shoot Seven Macaw at his dinner. Otherwise, glory would become just a matter of precious jewels, metals, riches and that was not good.

Here is the defeat of Vucub-Kaqix and his sons by the boys.

The boys (Hun-Ahpu and Xbalanque) laid in wait until Vucub-Kaqix went up the nance tree to eat its fruit. Hun-Ahpu took aim and shot Vucub-Kaqix with his blowgun, breaking his jaw. While running from the scene, Hun-Ahpu's arm was torn off by Vucub-Kaqix. The false lord returned to his wife, Chimalmat, to complain about his loose teeth and threaten to hang that trickster's arm over the fire.

For their part, the boys invoked a Great White Peccary and a Great White Coati (variously called Grandmother, Grandfather, and Doctors). The boys pretended to be the grandchildren of the Doctors when they returned to seek out the wounded Seven Macaw. These boy Doctors offered to treat the false lord by replacing his teeth with "ground bone". Reluctantly, Seven Macaw agreed. After pulling his teeth, the boy Doctors used white corn for ground bone. Seven Macaw lost his brilliance and died, as did his wife, Chilmalmat. Hun-Ahpu's arm was implanted in its socket and it healed.

Zipacna (Alligator) was bathing on the shore when the Four Hundred Boys (symbolically the stars in the Pleides) came by. Zipacna helped them with a post for their hut, showing his strength. The Four Hundred Boys quickly planned to kill Zipacna because they feared his power. They plotted to crush him with a log as he dug another hole for them. Zipacna realized this and dug a second hole for safety. The Four Hundred Boys began celebrating with sweet (alcoholic) juice when they thought they had killed Zipacna. Rather, he killed them by bringing their hut down upon them. The Hero Twins (the boys, Hun-Ahpu and Xbalanque) arrived to avenge the Four Hundred Boys. They tricked Zipacna into crawling on his back into a crevice in a canyon to obtain a crab to eat. However, the mountain crushed Zipacna and he turned to stone.

Carbracan (Earthquake) stamped his feet and mountains broke down. Heart of Heaven complained that Cabracan was trying to outweigh the sun. Hun-Ahpu and Xbalanque confirmed that this was an outrageous insult. The boys told Cabracan that there was a mountain in the East that he had not knocked down. Cabracan asked to be led to it. As they went, the boys shot birds with their blowguns, made a fire, roasted the birds, and coated one with clay. When Cabracan became ravenous at the smell of the cooked birds, the boys gave him the coated bird to eat. Soon Cabracan could hardly stand. He grew weak. He could do nothing. The boys tied his hands behind his back. He was bent over backward. His feet, neck, and hands were tied together. Then he was thrown down and buried in the ground.

## Comment

If the story of the three previous creations laid the mythological ground-work for the hierarchy of lords and rituals the gods would establish when the human work was complete, the defeat of Seven Macaw and his sons said, in effect, don't even think about challenging that hierarchy. You will be decisively defeated by the true sun and moon, and by extension, their rightful lordly descendants. Pay no attention to the riches and magical skills of imposters. Greatness lies with true lords not false lords. The measure of greatness is going to be the ability to trace your line, your ancestry back to the First Four Humans and thus to the Gods, the Maker and Former.

Ballgame symbolism is dramatically shown in the tying of hands, neck, and feet into a backward human ball. Cabracan's fate foreshadows the ball-game sacrifice of captives who will be tortured, exhausted, lose the ritualized game, tied up in a similar fashion, and rolled down the steep steps of a temple, perhaps to be buried at the "place of ballgame sacrifice".

Characters and events in the Popol Vuh often correspond to the move-ments of heavenly bodies, sealing the veracity of the story in cosmic cycles. Seven Macaw, for instance, was associated with the North and the Big Dip-per. In July, his star fell from the tree (hurricane season started). In October, he climbed back up the tree (hurricane season ended). The Four Hundred Boys symbolized the Pleiades (a handful of seeds) whose disappearance in the West marked the time to plant. Mayan kings and lords knew of these things and could tell them, and predict them, and point to them in the skies. What better authority could there be to rule on earth?

\* \* \* \* \* \*

The Popol Vuh now returns to a chronological line. We enter the heart of the myth. Ballplaying begins with Hunhun-Ahpu and Vucub-Hun-Ahpu (father and uncle of the Hero Twins) who meet their death in ballgame sacri-fice at the hands of the Lords of Xibalba. Blood Moon gives birth to the Hero Twins who, after several ballgames and many trials in Xibalba, fulfill their destiny and redeem their father.

# Hunhun-Ahpu (Maize God, First Father)

The narrators of the Popol Vuh propose a toast. They say, "… let us just drink to the telling …" of the story of Hunhun-Ahpu. They say they will tell part, just half, only the middle of his story. (ME)

Hunhun-Ahpu and Vucub-Hunahpu (One Hunter and Seven Hunter) were the sons of Xpiyacoc and Xmucane. Hunhun-Ahpu was married to Xbaquiyalo (Egret Woman) and they had two sons, Hunbatz and Hunchoven (One Monkey and One Artisan) who were great flautists, singers, writers, carvers, jewelers, silversmiths. Vucub-Hunahpu was not married and had no children.

Under the watchful eye of the hawk (messenger of the Gods), these four played ball and dice every day. They played on the road to Xibalba, which is the cosmic Milky Way, also the Underworld. Xibalba or the Underworld was beneath the earth plain in the day and above in the sky at night.

They played ball "over the heads" of Hun-Came and Vucub-Came (One Death and Seven Death), the highest Lords of Xibalba. These Lords of Death were very annoyed with the ball playing over their heads. Therefore, the Lords of Death summoned Hunhun-Ahpu and Vucub-Hunahpu to play ball in Xibalba. In their hearts, though, what the Lords of Death really wanted was the gaming equipment and playing costumes of Hunhun-Ahpu and Vucub-Hunahpu. These articles bespoke divinity.

Four owls (messengers of the Lords of Death) delivered the words of One Death, Seven Death, Pus, Yellow Bile, Bone Staff, Skull, Blood Gatherer, Filth, Misery, Hawk, and Leatherstrap as the Lords of Xibalba are called. Alighting above the ball court where Hunhun-Ahpu and Vucub-Hunahpu were playing, the owls instructed them to bring their playing gear and their "rubber ball".

Hunhun-Ahpu and Vucub-Hunahpu rushed off to inform their mother, Xmucane, of the summons. By this time, Xpiyacoc had died and so had Egret Woman, wife of Hunhun-Ahpu. Xmucane wept at the fate of her sons. They tried to console her. Then Hunhun-Ahpu advised his sons Hunbatz and Hunchoven (One Monkey and One Artisan) to remain at home and "… keep on playing the flute and singing, painting and carving; warm our house and warm the heart of your Grandmother." (AR) At that point, Hunhun-Ahpu and Vucub-Hunahpu left for Xibalba, taking their playing equipment but leaving the rubber ball tied up under the roof of the house.

The owl messengers guided Hunhun-Ahpu and Vucub-Hunahpu down a steep incline toward Xibalba. They did not fare well. They passed the Pus River and the Blood River. But they were defeated at the Crossroads of the Red Road, Black Road, White Road, and Yellow Road when they took the Black Road to Xibalba. They were defeated when they addressed wooden

31

manikins disguised as the Lords of Xibalba, saying "Greetings One Death and Greetings Seven Death". They were defeated when they accepted an invitation to sit on a bench that was really a hot rock. The Xibalbans shrieked with laughter at this, right down to their blood and bones. They were defeated in Dark House (House of Gloom), one of the tests of Xibalba. Given a torch and cigars already lit, they were told to return them whole in the morning. When they failed, they were told to hide their faces since they were to be sacrificed.

Hunhun-Ahpu and Vucub-Hunahpu were sacrificed and buried at the Place of Ballgame Sacrifice. However, Hunhun-Ahpu's head was cut off and set in the fork of a calabash tree. The tree immediately grew fruit and it became unclear where the skull of Hunhun-Ahpu was among the fruit. This so unsettled and amazed the Lords of Death that they said no one was to pick the fruit or even go near this tree.

## Comment

Admittedly, the case went badly for Hunhun-Ahpu and Vucub-Hunahpu. It could hardly have gone worse. They were out-smarted, humiliated, shamed, and killed by their tormentors. Yet, in the midst of disgrace, a pregnant possibility emerged when the tree came alive with fruit. A larger plan is sensed. The necessity of sacrifice and death is signaled. For the corn cannot grow unless the kernals (little skulls as the Mayans called them) are buried in the earth. Will Hunhun-Ahpu's skull (seed) bring new life in the face of death? Will those boy gods (Hun-Ahpu and Xbalanque, the Hero Twins) come to avenge Hunhun-Ahpu, just as they came to defeat the arrogant Vucub-Kaqix (Seven Macaw)? Of course, the answer is yes to these questions since Hunhun-Ahpu will eventually be resurrected by the boys as the Maize God.

Significantly, in this segment, Hunbatz and Hunchoven (One Monkey and One Artisan, the elder twins) are put on the fast track to second class status. They won't be major players. Their talents will be honored later but they will not be at the center of the blood ballgame ritual. It will be the younger set of twins, Hun-Ahpu and Xbalanque, who become the ballplayers. And the Hero Twin boys will not be born through Egret Woman since she has died. The mother of the Hero Twins awaits in the Underworld for her miracle impregnation.

# Blood Moon

One person in Xibalba resolved to disobey the mandate. This was the virgin princess, Xquic (blood of a woman, Blood Moon), daughter of Cuchumaquic (Blood Gatherer) who was a Lord of Xibalba. Blood Moon went unattended to the spot. She stood before the tree wondering whether she should pick its tantalizing fruit.

At that moment, the skull of Hunhun-Ahpu spoke to her from the tree, "What do you want with what are just skulls … You don't want them …" (ME)

"I do want them …" said Blood Moon.

The skull asked Blood Moon to stretch out her hand. The skull spat several drops of saliva into her palm. Immediately, Hun-Ahpu and Xbalanque were begotten in her belly. The skull explained that he had given her a sign. His face was without meat, without flesh, without image. But, the face of a lord, a sage, an orator does not die because it will live on in his sons and daughters, passed on in the saliva, the spittle. Thus, "I have done the same with you …" said the head of Hunhun-Ahpu. The skull assured Blood Moon that she would not die and instructed her to go up to the face of the earth. All of this "… was done by order of Huracan, Heart of Heaven." (LS)

Blood Moon did not go directly up to the face of the earth. She went home. In a few months, though, her father noticed her condition and was none too pleased. In response to her father's inquiries as to the identity of the father, Blood Moon said that she had known no man's "face". Her father and the rest of the Lords of Xibalba took counsel and decided to sacrifice this obvious "whore". They ordered the messenger owls to take her for sacrifice and to bring her heart back in a bowl.

On the way to be sacrificed, Blood Moon pleaded with the owls not to sacrifice her. She revealed how she became pregnant. The owls were convinced but said they had to have a substitute for her heart in order to satisfy the Lords of Death. Blood Moon replied, "Very well, but my heart does not belong to them." (AR) She told the owls to use the sap of a tree. She cut the cochineal tree (Red Tree, Blood Tree). Its sap ran red like blood. She gathered the Red Tree sap in a bowl and shaped it like a ball, like a heart. It was slippery and shiny like blood.

The owls returned with the substitute heart. One Death raised the heart with his fingers and it dripped with imitation blood. The Lords of Xibalba cooked the heart over a fire and savored its aroma. "They found the smoke of the blood to be truly sweet." (DT)

As the Lords of Xibalba were lost in reverie, the owls guided Blood Moon through a hole up to the face of the earth. The Lords of Death were blinded, were tricked by a "Maiden".

## Comment

The critical symbolic imagery of the ballgame is now set. Blood Moon's heart is the pool of blood in the bowl, the blood ball, the rubber ball. Hunhun-Ahpu's skull is the seed, the corn kernel, and later the ball as well. These images continually morph in the sacred art of the ballgame and in the playing of the game.

In cutting the Blood Tree to let its sap flow into the bowl, Blood Moon conjures the river of blood that runs naturally from her vulva (cave entrance, cleft in the mountain, watery underworld, birth place, womb). It is this mysterious flow of women's blood that is the unspoken desire of the gods of the Popol Vuh. The secret core of the myth and mythmakers is the desire to control the life force of all blood.

On the one hand, if the Lords of Death possessed Blood Moon's heart, then life would lose to death. There would be no cyclic renewal, no rebirth. But she tricked them. They will not have her real heart. The defeat of Hunhun-Ahpu promises to be temporary.

On the other hand, the desire of the Gods, through the skull of Hunhun-Ahpu, is the blood magic of Blood Moon, i.e., her power to birth Hun-Ahpu and Xbalanque (the true sun and moon). This God is not interested in an equal co-creative effort. His destiny is on the line. He will be fulfilled through Blood Moon under orders from Huracan, in his male aspect as the big guy upstairs. Blood Moon's heart is the rubber ball. But it's the Gods' ballgame.

Ominously, in the Underworld and soon on earth, unsanctioned sex leading to conception is seen to be "whorish" and worthy of death. Yet, the Maize God has apparent entitlement to the procreative powers of Blood Moon. He accomplishes this without normal human sexual intercourse. Gods never seem to procreate in the usual manner.

******

Recognizing the true nature of Blood Moon and her pivotal role in creation is the critical element in the essay I offer here. Unmasking the sexual implications of the Popol Vuh turns on the figure of Blood Moon. Three brief examples show how the sexual aspects of the Popol Vuh has been minimized or rather does not even appear on the radar of some notable writers.

The first is the work of Dennis Tedlock, preeminent translator of the Popol Vuh. As mentioned, Tedlock's 1996 translation remains the standard text. He updated it in part in a 2010 book titled 2000 Years of Mayan Literature. I can highly recommend both volumes but his take on Blood Moon in a chapter called "Blood Moon Becomes a Trickster" gives me grave misgivings.

Before his translation of the actual Popol Vuh text, Tedlock carefully describes the interaction in the underworld between the skull of One Hunahpu (First Father) and the maiden Blood Moon. He says that when Blood Moon fools the Lords of the underworld with a fake heart, she is seen in the story to "trick" the Lords. Tedlock notes that it is rare in mythology for a female to be considered a trickster. But that is where he leaves his interpretation thereby implying that Blood Moon is primarily a trickster.

To fail to see that Blood Moon represents the pro-active energy source that will bring the universe to life by seeking the dying seed is a fundamental omission. This clouded vision obscures how First Father and the Hero Twins capture Blood Moon's creative power for their aggrandizement and that of future Mayan kings.

A second example comes from the pen of Douglas Gillette who is a mythologist with a lengthy interest in Mayan myth and the co-author of King, Warrior, Magician, Lover a popular book on male archetypes.

In The Shaman's Secret (the Lost Resurrection Teachings of the Ancient Maya), Gillette delves into the "terrible beauty ... savagery and splendor" of blood ritual and art in Mayan myth. He suggests that the Mayans had "a kind of resurrection technology" effected through blood sacrifice. Importantly, he does see that blood "was the primary carrier of ch'ulel" or life force in Mayan myth. He also usefully catalogues the role of blood in myth and religion. Nonetheless, Gillette misses the sexual import of the Popol Vuh.

In his presentation of the exchange between First Father's skull and Blood Moon in the underworld, Gillette writes that the "maiden — fresh, courageous, and rebellious" stood before the tree where First Father's skull was hanging. She then "begged for her miraculous world-renewing conception." In response to the skull's insistence that she does not want a mere bone, Gillette writes that "We can almost see the eagerness and faith shining in her eyes as she says 'Yes, I do. I do want to make a world with you.'"

So we have Gillette's portrayal of Blood Moon as a perky little girl overwhelmed that the God has chosen her. This image is a far cry from the true face of Blood Moon as the source of ch'ulel (Chi) who sought the dead seed and gave it life.

Linda Schele affords us a third example. With co-author Mary Miller, Schele wrote in 1986 that "Blood was the mortar of ancient Maya life." As art historians of prodigious talent, the authors were uniquely suited to interpret the fabric of Maya life — sculpture, painting, ceramics, architecture, hieroglyphics. The hardback glossy edition of their book The Blood of Kings is filled with gorgeous photos and drawings that seemingly allow one to touch the art and smell the blood. This artistic sense informed their archeological, linguistic, and anthropological interpretations which have been uniformly praised.

Yet Schele never directly addressed the sexual dynamics in the Popol Vuh. Although she argued that the Mayan kingship system was founded upon and perpetuated through blood ritual, there was no acknowledgement that First Father and the Hero Twins usurped Blood Moon's power. Linda Schele passed away in 1998 and I can say only good things about her voluminous work even as I wish that she had tackled the sexual nature of Mayan myth head-on.

# Birth of the Hero Twins

When Blood Moon reached the face of the earth, she came to the house where Xmuncane (Grandmother) and the elder twins, Hunbatz and Hunchoven (One Monkey and One Artisan or One Howler), were living. Blood Moon announced herself to Grandmother, calling her "mother-in-law" and herself "daughter-in-law". Grandmother was very skeptical. After all, her sons had died in Xilbalba, said the Grandmother. Blood Moon answered that Grandmother's sons were not dead. Their faces were alive in what she carried, as the Grandmother would soon see.

Grandmother was unconvinced but relented in part. She told Blood Moon to go to the field of Hunbatz and Hunchoven and gather a big net of corn. This was a test. When she arrived, Blood Moon found only one clump of corn in the field. Despairing, she called upon the goddesses of rain, yellow corn, cacao, cornmeal, as well as Chahal, who was the guardian of the food of One Monkey and One Howler. Blood Moon pulled the silk tassel of an ear of corn without removing it from the clump. "Then she arranged the silk in the net like ears of corn and the large net was completely filled." (AR)

The animals carried Blood Moon's net of corn back to Grandmother's house. Grandmother rushed to the cornfield thinking that the whole field had been cleared. Instead, she found nothing missing, nothing picked. But, at the foot of the clump of corn where Blood Moon got the tassel was an impression in the ground of the full net of corn. This was read by Grandmother as a "sign of the net". Now she truly believed that Blood Moon was her daughter-in-law.

Hun-Ahpu and Xbalanque were born "suddenly" in the woods, in the mountains. Blood Moon gave birth but Grandmother was not there.

## Comment

The story continues to reveal the underlying source of creation. The boys are the seed of Hunhun-Ahpu but he came from Grandmother and the now deceased Grandfather. There is no creation or rebirth except from Grandmother and through Blood Moon. The seed is a life force that originates in the body of Grandmother and comes to birth in the blood of Blood Moon. Blood Moon's miracle production of corn (food of life and the god himself) with the aid of Xtoh, Xqanil, and Xkakau (goddesses of rain, corn, and cacao) further underscores her pivotal role in creation.

What Grandmother (foremost seer) saw in the "sign of the net" was likely the symbol of a woven reed Mat upon which a king sat. The miracle tassel that produced the net of maize symbolized the Maize God. Thus Blood Moon carried divinity.

# Hunbatz and Hunchoven (Singing Garden Boys)

In spite of Grandmother's assent to the magic of those whom Blood Moon carried in her belly, the new twins (Hun-Ahpu and Xbalanque) had a hard time of it. Grandmother was frustrated with those "crying loudmouths". They were put outside on the anthill and in the thistles. However, they just slept soundly. In truth, Hunbatz and Hunchoven wanted their younger brothers to die on the anthill and in the thistles. Being soothsayers, Hunbatz and Hunchoven understood the destiny of Hun-Ahpu and Xbalanque and the older brothers were envious, "flushed with jealousy".

While Hunbatz and Hunchoven played their flutes and sang all day, Hun-Ahpu and Xbalanque were made to grow up in the fields. When the younger brothers shot birds with their blowguns and brought them back to the house, Hunbatz and Hunchoven gave them nothing to eat. But Hun-Ahpu and Xbalanque knew their true rank and destiny, so they suffered this ill will.

Finally though, Hun-Ahpu and Xbalanque devised a way to overcome their older brothers. They went back to the house and explained to Grandmother that they needed their older brothers' help in getting some birds that were stuck in a tree. Hunbatz and Hunchoven were induced to climb a tree to fetch the birds. As they climbed, the tree grew taller and wider. They became frightened and could not come down. Hun-Ahpu and Xbalanque told their older brothers to loosen their belts and loincloths in order to move more freely. But, the loose ends turned into tails. Hunbatz and Hunchoven began to look like monkeys and they went swinging through the trees.

Hun-Ahpu and Xbalanque quickly confessed to Grandmother that there was bad news about their older brothers. What! Said the Grandmother. If you have hurt them, you have made me very unhappy, said the Grandmother. No, said the boys. Hunbatz and Hunchoven have changed into animals, into monkeys. We will call them with a song but don't laugh when you see them, Grandmother, said the boys.

"And in song, they called forth the 'Spider Monkey Hunter', as the tune is called. And they came back, One Monkey and One Howler, dancing as they came." (ME)

Grandmother saw them and could not help laughing at their silly faces and dangling things below their bellies. Hunbatz and Hunchoven immediately fled into the forest. Twice more, they were called in song and came back. On the fourth call, they did not come. They disappeared. They were lost in the forest.

Yet, it was said that the ancient people invoked them because they were great painters, carvers, singers. They did great things when they lived with their Grandmother and Mother.

## Comment

The story frames the conflict between Hunbatz and Hunchoven and their younger brothers, Hun-Ahpu and Xbalanque, as a case of sibling rivalry. Having no cause whatever, the older boys are simply jealous of their brothers. But, the effect of the story is to show that the old order of singing and dancing with Grandmother and Mother has passed. In other words, the mother centered village culture, although given credit for past works, must move aside (go back to the forest) in favor of the blood sacrifices of the ballplayers.

In the art of early villages throughout Mesoamerica, earthen figurines of unclad females were ubiquitous. These small "pretty ladies", as anthropologists originally termed them, were the most predominate art form and were found in large numbers in both burials and household sites. The most reasonable inference is that the early village cultures (cir. 1500 BCE - 300 BCE) were more egalitarian and woman centered than the subsequent divine kingship system.

Then, beginning at least several hundred years BCE, a shift occurred in Mesoamerican mythology (their story about themselves). This shift in the culture's mythology facilitated the movement from village culture to a highly stratified, patriarchal, urban culture. Like a computer graphic, one can almost see monumental temples rise literally on the spot of pre-existing villages, sending the village way of life scampering into the jungles and hills.

Once again in The Blood of Kings, Schele and Miller's insights are instructive. They spoke of Cerros on the coast of Belize, a farming, fishing and trading community in the first century BCE. Around 50 BCE, Cerros was razed of its buildings and "...stepped pyramids dominated by huge stucco masks in a dramatic new imagery were built; in this imagery, the primary elements of Classic Mayan iconography, the sun and Venus, appeared for the first time." And very recently, the discovery of spectacular, well preserved murals at the Mayan site of San Bartolo in the lowland jungles of Peten in Guatemala moved the dates of this transformative shift even further back. The murals are believed to be from about 100 BCE and depict a creation myth very similar to that in the Popol Vuh, including the birth of the cosmos, blood sacrifices, and the Maize God. A coronation scene shows a king descended directly from the Gods, thus sealing his divine right to rule. This means that monarchies were established in Mayan culture centuries before the "flowering" of Classic Mayan civilization (300 CE - 900 CE).

Hunbatz and Hunchoven were never forgotten. They remained the patron deities for lordly lines of scribes, painters, carvers. The makers of public art and architecture were essential to Mayan culture but now their function was to make art in the service of the state, in the service of the king, and not to console and entertain Grandmother. For this service, they were richly rewarded with wealth and position.

It may be that the authors of the 16th century text that is the Popol Vuh were members of a lineage connected to the images of Hun-Ahpu and Xbalanque ( Hero Twins, sacrificial ballgame warrior boys) while their adversaries were identified with Hunbatz and Hunchoven (singing garden boys). But, in terms of the political/sexual nature of Mayan culture, this is a distinction without a difference. Which lineage appeared to hold the reins of power was more akin to the usual non-choice between Republican or Democrat, Labor or Tory, etc. The spirit of the ballgame warrior boys completely dominated the singing garden boys (those ancients who sang with Grandmother/ Mother) from at least the first or second century BCE to the 16th century CE and the arrival of the Spanish conquerors.

******

So, the Maize God begat the Hero Twins through Blood Moon. And the blood ball in the coming ballgames will be Blood Moon's symbolic heart. The singing garden boys have been sent back to the forest. The way is clear for Hun-Ahpu and Xbalanque. Now the boys begin a process of self discovery which they will act out before Grandmother and Mother. This propels them on the path to Xibalba and the ballgames.

******

# The Path to Xibalba

The boys (Hun-Ahpu and Xbalanque) planted a garden but did nothing all day except shoot their blowguns. Nonetheless, their axe and mattock did the work of cultivation anyway. The boys "Returning at night … smeared their faces and hands with dirt so that Grandmother might be deceived into imagining that they had been hard at work in the maize field. But during the night the wild beasts met and replaced all the roots and shrubs which the brothers - or rather their magic tools - had removed. The twins resolved to watch for them on the ensuing night, but despite all their efforts the animals succeeded in making good their escape, save one, the rat, which was caught in a handkerchief. The rabbit and deer lost their tails in getting away." (LS)

The boys choked the rat until his eyes bulged. They burned the hair off his tail. The rat pled for its' life saying that planting maize was not the destiny for Hun-Ahpu and Xbalanque. Name it then, said the boys. The rat replied that the gaming equipment and rubber ball of their fathers, Hunhun-Ahpu and Vucub Hunahpu, was tied up under the roof of their house. However, Grandmother never told them about these things because of their fathers' misfortune.

The boys were extremely happy after they heard of the rubber ball. As a reward, they "gave" the rat his "food". From then on, the rat could gnaw away at waste and stored seeds, beans, cacao, etc.

A plan was hatched to obtain the ball equipment. The boys complained about the hot chili sauce they were eating. They persuaded Grandmother and Mother into going for water. Meantime, the rat climbed to the roof and chewed loose the ball equipment. The boys collected their prizes, hid them, and finished their chili. When Grandmother and Mother returned, the boys acted as if nothing had happened.

Very soon the boys swept out the court of their father and uncle and quite contentedly began playing ball. The Lords of Xibalba were doubly annoyed at the resumption of stomping over their heads. The Lords of Death determined to summon those shameless ballplayers to Xibalba for a game of ball. They had in mind the same fate that had befallen Hunhun-Ahpu and Vucub-Hunahpu.

As the boys continued to play, the owl messengers of Xibalba delivered the summons to Grandmother at the house. Grandmother was devastated because she realized that it was Xibalba again, summoning the boys to a fate like their fathers before them. She sobbed but told the messengers that the boys would come.

Grandmother "..dispatched a louse to carry the message to her grandsons. The louse, wishing to ensure greater speed to reach the brothers, consented to be swallowed by a toad, the toad by a serpent, and the serpent by the great bird Voc." (LS) Arriving at the ball court, Voc (the falcon) perched on the edge. When Voc cried out, the boys grabbed their blowguns and shot the falcon in the eye. Voc fell injured and the boys asked him why he had come. First heal me, said Voc. The boys took a piece off their rubber ball, "Blood of Sacrifice was their name for it". (DT) They put it on the falcon's eye and his sight was completely restored.

Voc vomited the snake. The snake vomited the toad. The toad could vomit nothing. Finally, the louse was discovered stuck in the toad's gum. The louse delivered the summons and the boys went straight to Grandmother.

The boys told Grandmother that they were going but they would leave her a sign. Both boys planted a reed, a cornstalk in the middle of the house. The sign of their death would be when the reed dried up. The sign of their rebirth would be when the reed sprouted. They gave Grandmother this sign and left.

## Comment

Here the distinction is further solidified. The boys, Hun-Ahpu and Xbalanque, are not gardeners. They have bigger fish to fry. They got some ball playing to do.

Though Grandmother wept for her sons and now her grandsons, everything goes through her. She was "notified" by Hunhun-Ahpu before his descent to Xibalba and the "summons" for Hun-Ahpu and Xbalanque came through her. She was the keeper in the universal house of the rubber ball and game equipment. And she is the keeper of the "sign" of the boys in what will be the most important food ritual in Mayan life — to burn incense before the dying and sprouting stalks of corn in the center of every Mayan household.

\* \* \* \* \* \*

Thus the boys are off to Xibalba. The incredible trials they will face in the underworld, their eventual victory over the Lords of Death through marvelous acts of magic and ultimately through self-sacrifice, and the triumphant resurrection of the bones of their father (the Maize God) may seem to be the centerpiece of the myth. But, for me, the pivotal action has already taken place. The essential dynamic and worldview of the narrative has been set. The Maize God and Hero Twins will act through Grandmother and the pool of blood, Blood Moon. The end result will be a line of lords who will take responsibility to properly "nurture the gods". The rest of the myth is fascinating but predictable. Who could doubt that the boys will defeat Death and raise their father? How else could there be the making of humans, the dawning itself, and the eventual radiant splendor of the K'iche lords? Although predictable in final outcome, the continuing story is gripping, especially in the telling of the ballgames. The bits about the pumpkin and the rabbit are my favorites.

\* \* \* \* \* \*

# Descent to Xibalba

The boys went down to Xibalba where they quickly began to turn the tables on the Lords of Death. They crossed canyons, the Pus River, the Blood River — crossing on their blowguns so as not to get their feet wet in those traps of Xibalba. In a clever, foresighted maneuver, they sent a mosquito (actually a hair from Hun-Ahpu's leg) on ahead to bite each of the Lords in turn. As each was bitten, he hollered "Ouch". The others said, "What is the matter One Death?" They were all named in this way. "Each one being denuded in the telling." (ME) Every Lord of Xibalba revealed his identity to the boys who were hiding nearby. When the boys entered the Lords' chamber, they passed the wooden figures dressed as Lords and started with the third seated saying, "Greetings One Death." The boys named every Lord without showing their own identities.

Next, the boys were instructed to "sit here". However, they were hip to the old hot seat trick and declined the command.

That night, the boys were sent to the House of Gloom (Dark House), the first test of Xibalba. Like their father and uncle before them, they were issued a burning torch and lit cigars and told to return them whole in the morning. The sentries were glad to report to the Lords of Death that the torch and cigars were burning all night. But, the boys substituted macaw feathers for the torch light and fireflies for the cigar tips. When the Lords examined the torch and cigars in the morning and found them whole, they were confounded. The Lords of Xibalba earnestly sought the identities of these highly unusual boys, asking where they came from. The boys played ignorant. They said they did not know where they came from.

The Lords were suspicious and frustrated. Nonetheless, they finally said to the boys, "Okay, let's go play ball."

## Comment

The power of names to reveal identity, origin and essence is the obvious lesson in the boys' naming of the mosquito bitten Lords. It would be difficult to overstate the importance of knowing and naming one's enemy — for no trickery or treachery can surprise you if you know the "face" of your enemy. The boys demonstrate this lesson with ingenuity and flair as they name evil (the Lords of Xibalba) and by naming them unmask their faces and sap their power. Conversely, they maintain their integrity and power by refusing to name themselves. They will name themselves but only at the right time. They are masters of the name game.

# Game One: Xibalba v. The Boys

The boys and Xibalba began the match by arguing over whose ball they should put in play.

The Xibalbans said the game should be played with their ball. The boys said "No". Their ball should be used. The Xibalbans insisted, "Use ours". The boys said "Okay". The Xibalbans said something to the effect that their ball simply looked like a painted marker. The boys said they thought it looked like a skull. Certainly not, responded the Xibalbans. Again, the boys said "Okay".

The game commenced and the Xibalbans' ball was stopped by Hun-Ahpu's ring (yoke, worn around the waist). The ball spilt open and out came the white knife of sacrifice which clanged and twisted around the ball court. The boys were outraged at the Xibalbans' treacherous intention to sacrifice them on the spot. The boys threatened to leave but the Xibalbans begged them to stay — offering to continue play with the boys' ball. At this point, the game prize was specified to be four bowls of flowers. When the boys' ball was "dropped in" and the game continued, the boys were equal to the Xibalbans in strength and skill "..since they only had very good thoughts." (DT)

Yet, the boys suddenly changed their strategy and allowed themselves to lose the game. The Xibalbans were very pleased and informed the boys that they must hand over the prize in the morning, knowing full well that the boys had no place to obtain flowers. Accepting their charge, the boys noted that they had to play ball at night too!

That night, the boys were taken to the House of Lances, where slashing knives were designed to cut them to pieces. The boys had a talk with the knives and on the condition that they would be given the flesh of animals to cut, the knives lowered their points and quieted.

After the knives stopped moving, the boys called upon the ants to go to the garden of One Death and Seven Death to snip and collect flowers for the prize. Earlier, the Xibalbans had instructed the guardians of their garden (whip-poor-wills) to be especially vigilant. But, these guardians just sang their night song from tree to tree and failed to notice the ants at work. The boys delivered the bowls of flowers in the morning. Pained and pale at the sight, the Xibalbans remonstrated the hapless guardians for permitting the flowers to be pilfered and they split the guardians' mouths. The Lords of Death were defeated and the mouth of the "whip-poor-will" remains split wide to this day.

## Comment

I nearly laughed out loud when I read of the Xibalbans and the boys contesting over which ball to put in play. I was reminded of countless arguments on playgrounds as a kid about whose football, basketball, or baseball we should use. It made me wonder if arguing over their balls is hard-wired in men. Yet, the ball was of utmost importance. The skull was useless without blood. Only the boys blood ball could bring new life.

The next lesson is that your opponent can be treacherous and may flagrantly disregard the rules of fair play. But the boys handled it. They deflected the evil of the white knife of sacrifice with deft play and gained the advantage with righteous indignation at the Xibalban treachery.

Later, when the boys' ball was "dropped in", they played with skill and strength because they had "good thoughts". Much is made nowadays of the positive mind set that an athlete must possess in order to vanquish an opponent whose mind set might not be quite as psychologically positive. The boys, it appears, were ahead of their time as early practitioners of the "mental game".

When the boys allow themselves to "lose", they manifest the critically important theme of self-sacrifice. This well chosen, timely apparent defeat of giving oneself up was a stratagem for obtaining ultimate victory rather than a true or final loss.

I think Game One should go into the win column for the boys. I say that because the game goes on through the night as the boys seek the prize of flowers. The game actually ends in the morning with the presentation of the captured prize, thus embarrassing the Xibalbans.

# Game Two: Xibalba v. The Boys

After putting the House of Gloom and the House of Lances behind them and beating the Xibalbans in Game One, the second game commenced for the boys.

The ball was dropped in and they played to a tie.

As each took leave for the night, the Xibalbans said, "Tomorrow morning, once more?" The boys said, "Okay" and left.

## Comment

Well, that was short and sweet. It seems the boys were playing for time, setting up their opponents for the critical match. There is nothing like a well played tie to prepare the stage and build the tension for the decisive struggle.

Prior to the start of Game Three, the boys will go through several more houses (tests) in Xibalba. They overcome the obstacles in each house before the following morning. My sense is that these remaining tests before the big game all take place in one night although I admit that the text indicates several nights instead of one.

So, Games One and Two are history. By my reasoning, the boys are up: one win, no losses, and one tie with the deciding match to come after a long, trying night.

# Game Three: Xibalba v. The Boys

At the conclusion of Game Two, the boys were ushered into the House of Cold where frost and freezing drafts were meant to kill them. But, they held back the cold and were alive when it dawned. The Xibalbans marveled at this.

Next, they were put in the House of Jaguars. Cleverly, the boys scattered bones in front of the hungry cats. When the sentries checked, they were pleased to observe that the boys had been torn to pieces by the jaguars. But, when the boys emerged from the House of Jaguars unscathed, the Xibalbans were confounded.

Then, the boys entered the House of Fire. But, the fire did not consume them. They were only singed a little. They were well in the morning. The Xibalbans lost heart when they saw the boys.

Finally, the boys were committed to the House of Bats. This was a frightful place where monstrous bats with teeth like knives screeched all night. The boys avoided them by sleeping in their blowguns. Then, in a premeditated move, one of the boys prepared to give himself up. Towards morning, the bats had calmed down. Xbalanque asked Hun-Ahpu if he could see whether it had dawned. Hun-Ahpu crawled to the end of his blowgun and peeked out. Immediately, a monstrous Death Bat swooped down and snatched his head off. Xbalanque became distraught at his brother's motionless body. Meanwhile, Hun-Ahpu's head went bouncing onto the ball court. The Xibalbans were beside themselves with glee at the sight of Hun-Ahpu's head.

Xbalanque, however, did not despair for long. He summoned the animals and bade them bring along their food so he could inspect it. The last to come was the coati who came pushing a pumpkin with his nose. The pumpkin became a substitute head for Hun-Ahpu. The Heart of Heaven came down into the House of Bats and made the brains for the pumpkin head. The face and eyes were carved as good as before. Even Hun-Ahpu, himself, conceded that the head was "good".

The boys conferred and Xbalanque suggested to Hun-Ahpu that he refrain from active ball playing. Xbalanque would take the action. Hun-Ahpu should confine himself to threats. At this point, Xbalanque instructed a rabbit to hide among the ball bags. And when the ball came, the rabbit must run away.

When it dawned, Game Three officially began. Both boys were good as new. The Xibalbans dropped in the ball and it was the head of Hun-Ahpu (the head the bat snatched off). The Xibalbans shouted that they won, that the boys were destroyed. Hun-Ahpu shouted back, "Punt the head as a ball." (DT) Not seeing any harm in this, the Xibalbans punted the head of Hun-Ahpu. Xbalanque stopped Hun-Ahpu's head with his yoke and sent it back hard to where it went among the ball bags. Right away, the rabbit took off, bouncing and hopping through the underbrush. The Xibalbans ran after the rabbit. The whole of Xibalba went careening after the rabbit, screaming as they went.

Hun-Ahpu strode to the ball bags, retrieved his real head, and secured it to his shoulders. The boys shouted to the Xibalbans to come back because they found the ball. The Xibalbans wandered back a little disorientated, wondering whether they had been seeing things. When play continued, Xbalanque dropped in the pumpkin head. Soon, the pumpkin head wore out and burst, sending its seeds flying in every direction over the ball court. Completely stunned, the Xibalbans weakly asked the boys where that ball had come from and how did they get it. In this way, the boys defeated the Lords of Xibalba.

## Comment

The boys are clear victors in Game Three. The method of defeat was visionary self-sacrifice. The agent of defeat was the seed of the God. The skull of the god is likened to the pumpkin. When the seeds come to light, the Lords of Death know they are defeated because the seeds signify new life. Death may be inevitable, but new life defeats death. As the pumpkin will rise from the planted seeds and the corn will rise from the planted kernels (little skulls), the God will continue to live through his children and the new corn. Later, when the boys resurrect and redeem the bones of their father (Hunhun-Ahpu), he will thereafter be recognized as the First Father/Maize God who is a seamless combination of God, man, and corn plant. The Mayan kings (including 18 Rabbit) revealed themselves to be the blood line of that universal tree (cornstalk, Maize God) through their timely re-enactment of these mythic ballgame events.

The ballgames are over and the tests of Xibalba are over. The boys have responded admirably. They are undefeated. They parried the worst that Xibalba could throw at them and, it would be fair to say, kicked butt in return. Even so, the story is far from over. The final transformative act of self-sacrifice awaits the boys. As one might expect, they see their destiny and rush headlong to fulfill it.

# The Oven

This is the story of the death of Hun-Ahpu and Xbalanque. This is their "memorial", their "epitaph".

The boys survived the tests of Xibalba, the voracious animals, the suffering, the ordeals. And they did not die. Yet, they foresaw their death and the instrument of their death — an oven.

The boys summoned two diviners, Xulu and Pakam, and gave them instructions about what to say to the Lords of Xibalba after the boys' deaths. When Xibalba asks you, said the boys, tell them it would not be good to dump our bones in a canyon or to hang our bones in a tree. Tell them it would be good to toss our bones in the water, in the river. But, tell them to grind our bones like corn is ground and then spread them on the water to flow between the hills both large and small.

While the boys were instructing Xulu and Pakam, the Xibalbans made a huge oven, filling it with a great quantity of firewood. Then the Xibalbans invited the boys for a treat, a drink and suggested they play a game of jumping over their drinks. This was a trick. They wanted the boys to fall into the oven.

The boys were not amused at the Xibalbans ploy and said they already knew their destiny. Hun-Ahpu and Xbalanque faced one another, grabbed hold of each other, and jumped straight into the oven. They died in the oven and Xibalba gloated.

When summoned by Xibalba, the diviners, Xulu and Pakam, did their work well. Thus, the boys "..bones were beaten to powder and thrown into the river, where they sank, and were transformed into young men. On the fifth day they reappeared like men-fishes, and on the sixth in the form of ragged old men, dancing, burning and restoring houses, killing and restoring each other to life, with other wonders." (LS)

Soon, word of the miracles performed by these ragged dancers traveled through Xibalba and reached the ears of One Death and Seven Death. These highest Lords of Xibalba desired to see for themselves whether the ragged beggars danced as beautifully as had been said. But the ragged old men (really those handsome boys in disguise) played hard to get. They said they were ashamed, not worthy to appear before such great Lords as One Death and Seven Death. It took much effort from the messengers of Xibalba to persuade the beggars to come to the house of One Death and Seven Death.

When they arrived before the Lords, the beggars bowed nearly to the floor in humiliation, in submission. The Lords pointedly asked the beggars where they came from, what mountain, tribe, mother, father. The boys divulged nothing. They said they did not know where they came from, that their mother and father died when they were young. The Lords gave up their questioning and entreated the beggars to proceed with their performance.

As the boys began, all of Xibalba gathered to witness the pageantry. The boys performed everything. They danced the Weasel, the Owl, the Armadillo. They sacrificed a dog and revived it. They burned the Lords' house and made it whole. They sacrificed a man and brought him back to life. One Death and Seven Death became more and more excited with every marvelous "dance". They implored the beggars to delight them by sacrificing themselves. It was then that Xbalanque sacrificed Hun-Ahpu. He cut off his arms and legs one by one. He cut off his head and it rolled away. He cut out his heart and held it up. The Lords of Death were intoxicated to the point of delirium at the sight of Hun-Ahpu's heart. Quickly, Xbalanque commanded Hun-Ahpu to rise. Immediately, Hun-Ahpu returned to life.

By now, One Death and Seven Death were consumed with desire for the "dance" of Hun-Ahpu. They pleaded with the boys, "Do the same, sacrifice us." With the offhand response, "Sure, you are Death, you should revive", the boys sacrificed One Death and did not revive him. Next was Seven Death and he shivered with fear when he saw One Death's fate. The Xibalbans humbled themselves in the presence of the dancers. But, the boys threw the grieving, sobbing Xibalbans into a deep canyon.

Thus, the boys defeated the Lords of Xibalba through miracles and transformation.

## Comment

The boys are not defeated by their own death because they see their death and know what they must do to win new life. Though death is inevitable, it is only a means to new life — for the face of a lord will live on in his son and the green corn will sprout from the old. But, it must be the right kind of death and the right magic must be done after death in order to bring forth new life.

The boys are models for facing death squarely. Their leap sends a message. Don't be tricked into your death by someone else's game (jumping over drinks). Don't grieve and sob in the face of death like the Xibalbans. Instead, take hands and dive into the oven because rebirth awaits.

However, make sure that your seed will be spread in the waters among the hills large and small before you jump. For it is the seed, the skull, the ground bone spread among the waters that will bring new life. The life, death, and rebirth of Gods, humans, and plants are intertwined, dependent upon one another. The skull is a corn kernel. The ground bone is flour. The human pregnant belly mirrors the earth mountain. The stream at the base of the mountain mirrors the flow of blood from the vulva. The pumpkin seeds and the corn kernels are spread in watery rivulets between furrows whose heights loom as large hills over the planted seeds. The God is likened to corn and humans will be made from corn flour and water. Eating tortillas is like eating God. The myth skillfully blends these images to weave a deeply textured tapestry. The story works as a way to explain the mysteries of life, death and rebirth because the underlying images are both common and magical.

It has been the dance of birth, life, death, and rebirth. The magic is in the dance. The ballgames are a dance. The sacrifices are a dance. The Gods are the dancers. Watch their footwork, their moves — aren't they pretty?

But, what happens to the winners and losers in this dance?

The conclusion to the exploits of the Hero Twins lies in a Revelation, a Resurrection, and an Ascension.

# Revelation

The boys had studiously refrained from revealing themselves during their entire sojourn in Xibalba. Having saved the power of naming until Xibalba was completely defeated, they now name themselves before the disgraced Xibalbans.

Heed our names and our fathers' names, said the boys. We are Xhun-Ah-pu (little Hun-Ahpu) and Xbalanque. You killed our fathers, Hunhun-Ahpu and Vucub-Hunahpu.

The boys berated the Xibalbans, telling them that they willingly had come to Xibalba and permitted their own torments in order to avenge their fathers. The Xibalbans were told to prepare for death. There would be no way out.

The Xibalbans threw themselves down, acknowledged that they had wronged the boys' fathers, and begged for mercy.

"Okay" said the boys. Then they pronounced the Xibalbans' fate.

The Xibalbans were denied any further greatness, any future worship of their day, and any descendants "born in the light". The game of ball was forbidden them. They were described as warlike, ugly as owls, inspiring evil and discord. Their faces were painted black and white to show their faithless nature. The Xibalbans "disappeared" through a loss of their assumed and illegitimate greatness.

Hun-Ahpu and Xbalanque were the architects of the Xibalban demise.

## Comment

When the boys revealed themselves before Xibalba in the glory and righteousness of their family position, it was the crowning moment in a mythology of good v. evil. The duality of good and evil was sharply drawn along the lines of the boys and their descendants versus outsiders and their descendants. To triumph over death, disease, and evil of every stripe, it will be necessary to be part of or somehow align oneself with the right family tree. And if true lords (those of the right tree) can show "Xibalban features" in a particular person or group, then any remedy is permissible — disappearance, killing. It's a mythology of Us v. Them in which the world is seen as a battle between some very good guys and some very bad guys.

# Resurrection

The resurrection theme comes in two parts. The first involves the living, dying, and re-sprouting corn, while the second concerns the re-constitution of Hunhun-Ahpu, the Maize God.

Grandmother remained at home the entire time the boys were in Xibalba. She burned copal before the reeds, the stalks planted in the middle of the house. The reeds sprouted and soon withered. This was a sign that the boys had died. Grandmother incensed the corn again, invoking the spirit of her grandsons. When the reeds grew a second time, this was a sign that the boys lived. Grandmother rejoiced. Grandmother worshipped the ears of corn and named them: Center of the House, Middle of the Harvest, Living Corn, Bed of Earth.

And there in Xibalba, the boys saw the face of their father. They had gone to the "Place of Ballgame Sacrifice". They wanted to put their father back together and he spoke to them. But, their father could not name all his body parts — only his mouth, nose, eyes. The boys consoled their father's heart and left him at the ball court. They confided to him that he would be worshipped first (First Father). His day would be kept first by those "born in the light".

## Comment

A late classic Maya bowl depicts Hunhun-Ahpu rising from a cleft in the back of a turtle (mother earth) as the Hero Twins assist him from either side. Hunhun-Ahpu is the Maize God whose head is elongated like an ear of corn with feathers like corn tassels flowing from his headdress. The cycle of life, death, and rebirth is complete. Everything and everyone who conspired against the cycle was defeated. The God is corn, the food of life.

In the ceremonial plazas of Mayan cities, the big (sometimes bloody) celebratory rituals were overseen and carried out by the big boys — the king and lords — and were recorded in fantastic displays of monumental art by the lineages of scribes and artists who served state religion. But they owed their very existence to Grandmother. After all, who gave birth to the Maize God, who had the authority to sanctify and name the ears of corn? Grandmother, of course. And Grandmother's ritual before the living, dying, and re-sprouting ears of corn would reach into every household in the land. In the center of every home, the humblest peasant incenses the dying corn and gives thanks to the new corn.

So, the boys avenged their father's death, put back his body as best they could, soothed his heart, and secured his place as the first to be prayed to. We have arrived at the moment of the boys' lasting glory.

# Ascension

The boys then mounted to heaven. The sun belonged to one and the moon to the other. When the first "dawn" came, they would be there in the sky.

The four hundred youths killed by Zipacna also climbed to heaven. They became the sky's stars.

## Comment

It is problematic whether Hun-Ahpu and Xbalanque are the sun and moon or whether they simply are associated with and control the sun and moon. In any case, the boys play a cosmic sky-god ballgame with the sun, moon, and stars. In the boys' final act, the story shows us that the sky is male. The mysterious moon that controls the tides belongs to one boy. The fiery sun that lights the earth belongs to the other boy. The starry constellations are hundreds of other boys.

Seems to be strong evidence as to why the men down on earth should be in charge.

\*\*\*\*\*\*

It may be useful, at this stage, to reflect on how far the story has progressed. And where it may go.

The myth began with the creation of the sky-earth, the plants and animals, and several failed attempts at creating the "human work". The Hero Twins enter the story prematurely in order to defeat the imposter Seven Parrot and his sons, Zipacna and Cabracan. Then the story returns to a strict chronology with the ball playing and death of Hunhun-Ahpu, the Maize God, in Xibalba. It continues with the miracle birth of the Hero Twins (Hun-Ahpu and Xbalanque) from Blood Moon. The Hero Twins grow up and chase their elder brothers (Hunbatz and Hunchoven) into the forest. Thus the singing and gardening way of life is replaced by the sacrificial ballgame warrior way of life. The Hero Twins discover the ballgame equipment of their father. Like their father, they are summoned to play ball in Xibalba. But, they turn the tables on the Lords of Death by passing the tests and beating them in the ballgames. The apotheosis, though, is the self-sacrifice of the Hero Twins in the oven and their rebirth in the water. After their rebirth, the Hero Twins complete an ultimate triumph over the Lords of Death through magic and song, especially the dance of heart sacrifice. At last the boys reveal their identities, resurrect their father, and ascend to the sky as the sun and moon.

An incredible amount of drama has occurred but there is more to come. After all, humans have yet to be made and the sun has yet to "dawn".

To quote a famous seer of the baseball diamond, "It ain't over 'til it's over." But the Hero Twins no longer appear in the story. Their job is done.

Shortly, humans will be made from corn and water - - the first four mother-fathers. These four and the K'iche people receive their gods and are given ritual instructions by the gods. There are troubles and travails for the K'iche people until the star (Venus) that is the sun carrier is seen. Soon it "dawns" for all the tribes. The K'iche establish their first citadel (mountain stronghold) and defeat rival tribes. Eventually, death comes to the first four mother-fathers but they leave a sign, a memorial for their remembrance. It's the "sacred bundle".

At this juncture, the story turns toward the history side of the mythistory of the K'iche people. In a trip to a city in the East, several K'iche lords receive the "emblems" of lordship. The K'iche move over time to different citadels. Their numbers increase and their power grows as they defeat rivals. Blood sacrifice of captives accompanies these victories as does increasing amounts of tribute paid to the K'iche by defeated enemies. As their fiery splendor manifests, new lineages are founded from the many vassels. The magical prowess and military genius of famous lords is highlighted. The culmination of the story is the sequential naming of the high Lord (mother-father) of each lineage of the K'iche, beginning with one of the first four mother-fathers and concluding with the generation alive at the time of the writing of the Popol Vuh.

The larger import of this close look at the Popol Vuh is that the sexual ballgame mythology that climaxed in the Hero Twins rise to the heavens will have its effect on the cultural dynamics of real people. This, I think, has relevance for our ballgame mythology.

In a posthumously published book, Linda Schele assessed the Mayan classic ballgame. "The ballgame was the metaphor for life and death .. It was sometimes played for the joy of the sport .. The ballgame was also a metaphor for war, in which great states and heroes strove for victory against enemies .."

Sounds familiar to me.

# First Four Mother-Fathers

Heart of Heaven, Heart of Earth, Plumed Serpent, Bearer and Begetter, Modeler and Maker were once more in council, in the dark, in the night. Thinking, searching for the makings of the human flesh. Because dawn was near. Those who were to nourish and sustain the Gods must be made.

It was the animals who discovered the yellow ears of corn and the white ears of corn in a beautiful land of abundant food called Split Place. Cat, coyote, parrot, crow showed the way.

The corn was ground. Xmucane did the grinding nine times. Water was used for the blood. The rinse water from her hands became fat when shaped by the Bearer and Begetter. This was the making of the first mother-father. Only corn, staple foods were used for the flesh of the first fathers, the four men.

Their names were Balam-Quitze (Tiger with the Sweet Smile), Balam-Agab (Tiger of the Night), Iqi-Balam (Tiger of the Moon), and Mahucutah (Not Right Now). They had neither father nor mother, neither were they made by the ordinary agents in the work of creation. Their creation was a miracle of Hurakan.

However, these men turned out too perfect. They saw too far. They knew too much. They were like Gods. So Hurakan breathed a cloud over their eyes, limiting their vision as a mirror that is breathed upon.

Then the four men slept, and four women were made, Caha-Paluma (Falling Water), Choimha (Beautiful Water), Tzununiha (House of Water), and Cakixa (Water of Parrots). These women became the wives of the men, women of the highest status, who gave birth to the tribes.

## Comment

At last, the human work was complete. The mountain cleft where bitter water flowed, where the white and yellow corn was found is suggestive of the fullness of a pregnant belly and of the strong smelling flow of blood and water from the opening at the base of the belly that precedes birth.

There is a fundamental shift in consciousness once again in the creation process. Although Xmucane (Grandmother, Bearer) ground the corn, a sleight of hand awards the Gods credit for creation. In four lines, the myth moves from female-male to male. There is the shaping of the first mother-fathers, who are then termed the first fathers, the four men. The effect of creating the mythological male mother-fathers is to justify the patriarchal framework of Mayan society where place and worth are set by one's rank in the male line. The name of the game will be to directly trace your ancestry back to one of the first fathers.

The initial ability of the first fathers to see like Gods brings us back to the rationale for the Popol Vuh. It is the Popol Vuh that wipes clean the cloudy mirror of the first fathers' eyesight and allows them and their descendants to see future events and past creations.

But the Popol Vuh accomplishes the opposite. It obfuscates the vision of a garden tended by singers, carvers, dancers — those who warmed the heart of their Grandmother. It overlays the garden with the specter of an avenging duo who create a warrior culture. The Popol Vuh repackages the symbols of birth, life, death, and rebirth into a ballgame that discards the blood magic of menstruation and the birth process in favor of the counterfeit magic of blood sacrifice.

* * * * * *

When Grandmother ground the corn nine times, she signaled the foundation of time — the human gestation period of nine months, as well as the nine month growing season of maize. Over and over again the nine month cycle is repeated, in the levels of the underworld, in the levels of monumental pyramids, and in the Tzolkin, the 260 day calendar of 13 months of 20 days each at the heart of Mayan time. And while it is accepted among the broad spectrum of commentators on Mayan calendrics that the natural rhythms of gestation, agriculture, and the lunar cycles appear to be the origin of the Mayan calendar system, the import of this understanding is often lost.

For example, archaeoastronomer Anthony Aveni addresses the question of the origin of the Mayan calendar in The End of Time (the Mayan Mystery of 2012).

Aveni notes that the Tzolkin appears to be unique to the Mayans, that it "is the centerpiece of the Mayan calendar system", and that it continues in use today in "remote areas." He then asks, "But why 260?"

Answering his own question, Aveni posits, "…could 260 have emerged as a seminal number because it connotes something natural in human experience?" (ie. The 266 day average human gestation period). He adds that "… Maya women still associate the Tzolkin with human gestation … and time their term by the moon, counting nine months of the phases." Continuing, Aveni says, "In some parts of the Yucatan they still say that the moon draws 'nine bloods' away from the pregnant mother to give to her the newborn."

An epigraph from Helen Neuenswander on the K'iche Maya in 1981 expands on this idea. Neuenswander reported that "…the Maya layman has retained, from earliest times, a high level of proficiency in the art of telling time and that the unit upon which his most exacting calculations are based is now, as then, the lunar cycle." Further, these modern Maya described each day "…precisely in terms of what the moon looks like at night and where it appears at dark or dawn…" and "…the position of the moon determines the rainy and dry seasons." In addition, "Pregnant women (in the study) who claim to be unable to count and measure time in the Western manner are able to give precise accounts of the progress of their term of gestation by reference to the moon, which they call 'our grandmother'." (HN from PR)

Aveni summarizes, "… the birthing cycle is a fair approximation to the length of the basic agricultural cycle in most areas of the Mayan world. So 260 neatly ties two fertility cycles together, those of women and earth."

I wholeheartedly agree with Aveni's summary thus far. Unfortunately, he goes on to minimize and entangle the notion he just put forward. Setting aside the natural rhythms of women and earth, he offers "I have long suspected that there may be astronomical reasons behind the origin of 260." He looks to the cycles of Venus and to the zenith points of the passage of the sun for possible connections to the number 260.

As for Venus, Aveni says that "...the average interval of the planet's appearance as morning or evening star is 263 days." He then suggests a correlation between the Venus cycle, the eclipse seasons, and the 260 day tzolkin saying that "...the average duration between successive halves of the eclipse season, 173.5 days, commensurates with the Tzolkin in the perfect ratio of three to two."

Aveni then writes, "If this seems contrived ..."

Here I must again wholeheartedly agree with Aveni but not for the reason he may wish. To make such a statement, a writer is almost always admitting through the back door that a contrivance may be afoot. It is tantamount to an admission against interest (his own statement).

Aveni completes his thought stating that "...there is evidence ... that the Maya used the Tzolkin to predict when Venus would appear and when eclipses would occur." He finds, "...certain named days in the 260 day count were tagged as unlucky because they marked a period of inauspicious events, such as eclipses." Aveni concludes, "The three-to-two commensuration between the eclipse cycle and the Tzolkin guarantees that certain days particularly vulnerable to the occurrence of eclipses will fall in clusters at intervals one third of a cycle (about 120 days) apart in the Tzolkin."

Although Aveni strings together several numerical threads, it seems a stretch. The Mayan calendar is a base 20 system and numerous permutations of 20 may be discovered within the calendar cycles but have no bearing at all upon the calendar's origin.

Secondly, Aveni speaks of the sun's zenith points within a narrow band 100 miles wide at about 14.5 degrees north latitude. This narrow swath of land is close to the Mayan cities of Copan and Izapa. The sun reaches its zenith when it is directly overhead at noon and casts virtually no shadow. In the area described by Aveni, this happens twice in a solar year (360+5, called a Haab), once in May (rainy season) and once in August (first harvest). Aveni notes that in this particular bandwidth, the sun spends 105 days north of 14.5 degrees between the May zenith and August, then spends 260 days south of 14.5 degrees between the August zenith and May.

However, although the solar zeniths are very important to the Maya, their connection to the number 260, especially on calendar origins, is tenuous at best. Aveni's 105 to 260 ratio occurs only in what he calls the "ideal latitude", described above. When the zenith cycles throughout Mesoamerica from 14 to 20 degrees latitude are examined, the 260 figure ranges significantly from 255 to 301. These are numbers taken from a table of solar-zenith passages compiled by Aveni himself in another context.

Finally, Aveni asks again, "So where did 260 come from."

He answers, "My best guess is that the sacred count of days acquired its importance when some enlightened Maya day keeper realized that the number 260 brought together many things."

Really?

Although the weight of the evidence for the origin of the Tzolkin points solidly to the rhythms of human gestation (amply supported by the direct testimony of living Mayans) and to the growing cycle of maize, Aveni conflates his astronomical calculations with the stronger evidence. In so doing, he gives equal weight to both and loses the thread of the original and enduring sense of Maya time. This is a critically important loss because it means that he cannot see how Grandmother Time, like Blood Moon, is circumscribed within the Popol Vuh to justify the authority of Mayan kings.

Blood Moon, the creative life force, gave birth to the universe, and the seed lived through her. Grandmother, the day keeper behind all others, fashioned the human work and framed time. But it will be the king standing atop the nine tiered temple who controls the ballgame of life and death and the kingdom.

******

So, with the forming of the first four mother/fathers, the stage is set for the true birth of the people born in the light, those who will nurture the Gods. It is just before dawn for the K'iche.

******

# Pre-Dawn

The sun had not risen but the tribes multiplied in the East. The K'iche had not yet found their home citadel. There were three K'iche lineages that began from the four mother-fathers. And there were nine houses in each lineage. There were also many secondary tribes. They became numerous in the pre-dawn. They fasted and prayed for the dawn.

When no sun came, they grew uneasy. So they set out for Tulan Zuiya (Seven Caves) and there Gods were given to the first fathers. Balam-Quitze received the God, Tohil. Balam-Agab received the God, Avilix. And Mahucu-tah the God, Hacavitz. The Gods were hoisted away in the backpacks of the first mother-fathers. It was representations of the Gods.

The God, Tohil, gave the K'iche the gift of fire to keep them from the pre-dawn cold. When the fire went out in a rain storm, Tohil gave the K'iche fire again by turning, pivoting in his shoe. Trembling with cold, the other tribes begged the K'iche for a bit of their fire. The first mother-fathers asked Tohil for advice.

Tohil said that if the other tribes wanted fire, they must be willing to be "suckled" under their arms, on their sides. (This meant heart sacrifice). For the gift of fire, the tribes agreed. They were sacrificed in honor of Tohil. Then Tohil spoke to the four mother-fathers again, saying they must leave Tulan for it was not their home. And they must bleed their ears and elbows in thanks to their God. This was done by the mother-fathers.

The three K'iche lineages and the secondary tribes camped along the road as they traveled from the East. Wandering, they faced innumerable hard-ships, high mountains, and a journey across waters. On one mountain, Tohil had to warn them to hide their Gods from theives and plunderers. At length they reached a mountain that they called Hacavitz, like their God. Here they rested because they had been instructed that they should see the sun.

## Comment

Though the K'iche were waiting for the dawn, the first sunrise, it appears that their "historical" birth as a people was tied to the established culture of Teotihuacán (Tulan Zuiva, Seven Caves) either directly or through a satellite city. From this culture in the East (central Mexico), the K'iche obtained the primary symbols of their culture, i.e. the Gods who instructed them and the emblems of their offices.

The basic formula for blood sacrifice was outlined by the God, Tohil. The secondary tribes, the outsiders, the enemies of the K'iche will be "suck-led" (have their hearts cut out) in subjugation before the Gods and the lords of K'iche and to whom the defeated tribes will pay a continuing monetary tribute. As for the lords of K'iche, they were provided a list of body parts to bleed in thanks before their Gods.

# Dawn

The morning star, Venus (herald of the sun), came up first. The mother-fathers uncovered the incense that had come with them from the East. They burned their copal in the direction of the rising sun, dancing and weeping with happiness as they did.

The sun appeared. Animals and men were transported with delight. All the celestial bodies were now established. The animals, tribes, and sacrificers knelt down in worship as the sun rose for all the peoples.

But the sun's face was unbearable. It's heat dried up the moist earth. The K'iche Gods (Tohil, Avilix, Hacavitz) were turned to stone. And the animal icons were also turned to stone. These were the puma, jaguar, snake, fer-de-lance. However, White Sparkstriker, White Demon was not turned to stone. He took care of the petrified ones, hiding them in trees.

Now, in the present days, the sun in the sky is only a mirror reflection of his former self. It is said, though, that the K'iche people may never have had their "day", their power, if the sun had not turned the voracious biting animals into stone.

The K'iche were not many when the sun, moon, and stars showed themselves on the mountain called Hacavitz. Still they were happy in their citadel and began to increase. They lamented, though, for the "brothers" who were lost or left behind after leaving Tulan Zuiva. The loss weighed heavily upon them. Languages had become different and the name of the God changed between the separated tribes. The former unity was gone. This separation would never be righted in the future.

Then Tohil spoke to the mother-fathers and warned them that other tribes were very jealous of their Gods. Because of this, Tohil instructed the mother-fathers to kill female deer and birds, set the deer pelts aside, and give the Gods the blood to drink. To fool the envious tribes, it should be said that the Gods were in the deerskin bundles. So, the deer and birds were hunted and their blood anointed the mouths of the Gods, who spoke as soon as they tasted the blood.

Later, the mother-fathers brought blood from their ears and elbows before Tohil, Avilix, Hacavitz. When the Gods had drunk, they became as boys and told the mother-fathers that their salvation lay in subjugating many tribes. The permission for this came from Tulan when they received their Gods.

## Comment

The manifest destiny of the K'iche people to defeat neighboring tribes came from Gods of stone who had their tongues loosened by the blood of female deer, birds, and blood from the ears and elbows of the mother-fathers. A heavy message in a heavy medium. And it all came from Tulan, back East — the Gods, the copal, the instructions, the authority for war.

The question arises. When did the "first" sunrise occur? Obviously, a great deal transpired in the darkness before the official dawning for those "born in the light". Adrian Recinos notes that Friar Francisco Ximenez concluded that the dynasty of the K'iche kings lasted 480 years, which for

Ximenez would make the K'iche "dawn" to be 1054 CE. This was close enough to Recinos' calculations for him to concur.

It is very interesting that Mayan scholarship suggests that the essence of the Popol Vuh is at least 1500 years older than the K'iche "dawn". In discussing the meaning of the Mayan ballgame, Linda Schele and Peter Mathews say, "… our best information about the ballgame comes from the Popol Vuh of the K'iche, a seventeenth century transcription of a Creation myth that appeared in the archaeological record by 400 BCE." Recent findings at San Bartolo in the lowland jungle of Peten in Guatemala may push this date even further back.

There is a crucial point to be made about the animal deities (icons) turned to stone. Adrian Recinos remarked that the K'iche may not have realized their "day", their "power" if the animal icons were not turned to stone by the sun. He said, "The transformation of the animals into stone, according to Chavero, is a symbol of the change of religion, their abandoning the old animal nature cult for the worship of the heavenly bodies." This observation adds weight to the suggestion that the singing garden boys were replaced by the sacrificial ballgame warrior boys. The "birth" of the K'iche nation meant the death of nature religion. Although this process was actually well underway nearly 2000 years before the K'iche "dawn" when the Mayan kingship system had already begun to take root.

Further along this line of thought. The K'iche have the sun, the dawning. They have Gods who will guide them on to victory (provided the Gods are "nurtured"). They are beginning to increase on their citadel. But, they mourn a loss. There used to be unity of purpose. Now there is separation. There used to be a shared language. Now there are many. There was one name for the God. Now there are other names for the God. Jealousy and envy have to be guarded against. The pre-dawn past was described as cold. People were hungry and wandered around in animal skins for clothes. But, in spite of that characterization, there appears to be a regret for the loss of a more peaceful, harmonious time before they received the word from back East.

When the sun turned the Gods and animal icons into stone, the Gods assumed the form they would have in Mayan ritual life. What form they had in the mother-fathers' backpacks may not be clear, but from now on, the Gods will be stone — intricately carved and placed on pedestals. Though they are stone, the Gods can fairly be described as bloodthirsty.

# Killing of the Tribes

The killing of the enemy tribes commenced.

Buoyed by Tohil's reminder that they had permission for many victories, the K'iche started kidnaping one or two people at a time along the road.

The victims were sacrificed before Tohil and Avilix and their bones placed on the road to give the tribes the impression that jaguars had been at work. Soon, the tribes realized that the K'iche, the worshippers of Tohil and Avilix were the cause. The tribes tried to follow the tracks of the K'iche but clouds, rain, mud, mist prevented them.

However, when the Gods of stone (Tohil, Avilix, Hacavitz) went out walking as spirits, they manifested as young men. These "boy-gods" often bathed in a river and were seen by the tribes — yet they quickly vanished.

These enemy tribes held council and devised a plan to defeat or capture the Gods of the first mother-fathers. The lords of the tribes chose two radiant maidens from their daughters and instructed them to wash clothes in the river where the spirits of the K'iche Gods bathed. When the boy-gods came, the maidens were to undress, entice them, and give themselves to these Gods. The maidens would be killed if they failed to offer themselves. They were to bring back a token, a sign that the boy-gods knew their "faces".

The maidens were truly beautiful when they undressed themselves, but the Gods did not lust after them or violate them as the tribes had intended. Instead, the boy-gods questioned the maidens and discovered their intention. They told the maidens to wait a little while for their sign before returning. Then the Gods directed the mother-fathers to make three capes with images of the Gods' essence stiched or painted inside.

The maidens presented the finished capes to their lords and the latter tried them on for size. They were pleased at these signs of the "sin" of the Gods. The first cape with jaguar inside fit well and the second cape with an eagle felt good. But, the third cape had hornets and wasps inside that stung the lord, who screamed in anguish. Thus, Tohil defeated the enemy tribes.

The lords of the defeated tribes reprimanded the maidens, called them devils and whores, and thought of them in that way from then on.

## Comment

Misogyny dramatically reared its head in this segment. The Gods (and those who would be God-like) will not fall for lusty maidens at the river bank. What could possibly come from such activity except a lack of focus on nurturing the Gods, unwanted pregnancies, and unarranged marriages. No, that will not do for God nor man.

These wanton women came from outside the line of the first mother-fathers, the K'iche root. The lords of other tribes may stoop to forcing their daughters to offer themselves to strangers and then turn them out as whores afterward. The daughters of the K'iche are different. They will not have sex on the river bank but will wait for the proper marriage to be arranged and the right price paid. The fate of the maidens stands as a stark example to K'iche daughters of what would befall them if they acted like temptresses.

# Storming the Citadel

After they failed to defeat the K'iche Gods through debauchery, the enemy tribes held council once more. Since the K'iche were still small in number in those days and were clustered around the citadel of Hacavitz, the tribes decided to storm the citadel because the tribes were greater in number. The mother-fathers anticipated the attack and constructed a fortification around their mountain top. They made wooden figures, decorated them with warrior markings and placed them on the stronghold walls to frighten the enemy. But, a spy for the tribes confirmed that the K'iche number was small and augmented only with the wooden warriors.

Tohil was asked for his advice. Because the mother-fathers had nurtured him, Tohil said he would explain how to defeat the tribes. He told them they should fill four huge gourds with hornets and wasps and put them at the corners of the citadel.The tribes launched their attack. There were countless thousands of them. They charged up the side of the mountain, armed to the teeth, shouting, whooping, howling, banging on drums. They reached the very edge of the walled enclosure. Just then, the gourds were opened. Swarms of hornets and wasps, like billows of smoke, poured out of the gourds and attacked the invaders. The insects stung their eyes, ears, noses, mouths, arms. The tribes fell down, numb from the stings. Now they hardly felt the K'iche arrows and axes. They could be killed with sticks. Even the women joined in the killing. As the K'iche prepared to finish them off, the tribes begged for mercy. The K'iche relented but said that from then on and forever, the tribes would be their subjects and pay tribute.

## Comment

To the victors, go the spoils. The K'iche right of tribute from the lesser, defeated tribes began in the time of the first mother-fathers. Here is a mythology of victory, as told by the victorious party.

# Death of the First Mother-Fathers (Long Count and 2012)

Happy, at last, on their mountain after the defeat of the tribes, the first mother-fathers nonetheless indicated that their death was nearing. They called their descendants together to hearken unto their last counsels. In the anguish of their hearts, they sang the Kamucu, the song "We See", that they had sung when it first became light, dawn. They took leave of their wives and sons, one by one. And suddenly they were not. But in their place was a huge bundle, which was never unfolded.

The "bundle" was a remembrance of the being of the first mother-fathers, though its contents stay hidden. The wives, sons and daughters of the first mother-fathers immediately burned sacred resins before the Majesty Enveloped, Bundle of Greatness, Shrouded Glory, Bundle of Flames.

Shortly, the sons of the first mother-fathers (those next in line) followed the last words of advice from their fathers. They traveled to the East and received their titles of office and insignia of royalty from Lord Naxit, the king of a mighty city (Copan or Teotihuacan?). The sons were invested with the titles of Ahpop and Ahpop-Qamha (the ones with the right to sit upon the "mat" of supreme authority). They were awarded the royal insignia: canopies, bone flutes, throne, snail shells, jaguar claws, deer feet, yellow powder, beads, parrot feathers. When these sons returned to Hacavitz, they revealed their signs of glory and lordship to all the K'iche and the tribes. They also brought the writing, the scripture of Tulan.

## Comment

If the Popol Vuh is a mythology of victory, it is equally a mythology of limited access to the central articles of faith. The sacred bundle is the container of the essence of the first mother-fathers. Next to the tree stones of the Gods, it is probably the most sacred artifact in Mayan religious practice. But its contents are unknown, mysterious. It will be handled only by the highest ranking lords. The bundle will not be available to ordinary people for examination, touching, inspiration. The high lords of K'iche will be the intermediaries for the people.

The titles of high office, the insignia of lordship, and the writing from Tulan were critically important additions to K'iche rank and ritual. They had their Gods, but with the birth of sons and a growing population, offices and rankings needed to be spelled out. The titles and insignia would show who was who. With the "second generation", we seem to be witnessing the birth of the nation/state and time itself takes on an added dimension.

Perhaps it is safe to say that, with the foundation of the Mayan state, the Long Count now rises to place of prominence in the affairs of Mayan politics and culture. Like a majestic monumental temple built upon a previous temple in the center of a Classic Period Mayan city, the Long Count was constructed upon the shoulders of the Tzolkin, Haab, and Calendar Round. It is the Long Count, though, that gives us 2012. But to reach 2012, the path goes through the Tzolkin, Haab, and Calendar Round, then to the Long Count.

Once again, as mentioned earlier, I cannot delve deeply into the mechanics of the Mayan calendar nor reproduce hieroglyphic images. My limited purpose here is to provide a context for commenting on 2012. With that in mind, I'll outline the Tzolkin, Haab, Calendar Round, and Long Count in short form. Don't be surprised, though, if this is difficult to follow. Most professional "Mayanists" agree that the details of the Mayan calendar can drive them to distraction.

**Tzolkin:** The Tzolkin is Grandmother's sacred count of days. Twenty day names make a month. The day names are preceded by thirteen numbers. Thirteen of these twenty day months constitute the 260 day Tzolkin. Each day is shown as it's own glyph and has special characteristics, powers, auguries. The thirteen numbers are represented by a dot for one and a bar for five. The Mayans use glyphs but non-Mayans write in Roman numerals and Latin script. In the Yukateko version (most commonly employed), the days are named:

1 Imix (water lily)
2 Ik' (wind)
3 Ak'bal (darkness)
4 K'an (corn)
5 Chukchan (celestial snake)
6 Kimi (death)
7 Manik' (deer)
8 Kamat (venus)
9 Muluk (jade)
10 Ok (dog)
11 Chuwen (monkey)
12 Eb (rain)
13 Ben (green)
1 Ix (jaguar)
2 Men (eagle)
3 Kib (wax)
4 Kaban (earth)
5 Etz'nab (flint)
6 Kawak (storm)
7 Ajaw (ruler)

The next month of 20 days continues with the repetition of the day names preceded by numbers from where the previous month concluded, i.e., 8 Imix, 9 Ik' and so on until it all comes round again to 1 Imix and the conclusion/beginning of the 260 day cycle.

**Haab:** The Haab is the 360 + 5 day solar calendar of 19 months. The first 18 months have 20 days each. The 19th month has only 5 days and these days are considered unlucky. Each month has its own glyph and its special divinatory aspects. A number glyph from 0 to 19 precedes every month and shows the number of the day within the month. The zero is not written with the glyph for zero but rather as a glyph called Chum. This Chum day is the "seating of the month". In the Yakateko version (western writing), the Haab reads:

(0 to 19)  Pop (mat)
    "      Wo (black conjunction)
    "      Sip (red conjunction)
    "      Sotz' (bat)
    "      Sek (skull)
    "      Xul (dog)
    "      Yaxk'in (new sun)
    "      Mol (water)
    "      Ch'en (black storm)
    "      Yax (green storm)
    "      Sak (white storm)
    "      Sej (red storm)
    "      Mak (enclosed)
    "      K'ank'in (yellow sun)
    "      Muwan (owl)
    "      Pax (planting time)
    "      K'ayab (turtle)
    "      Kumk'u (granary)
(1 to 5)   Wayeb (unlucky)

A date in a Haab month would begin with the Chum glyph in front of the month name (the seating). Next comes 1 through 19 before the month name, i.e., 1 Wo, 2 Wo, 3 Wo, etc. The following months continue this formula until the 18 months of 20 days and the month of 5 days complete the 365 day solar year. Then the cycle renews.

**Calendar Round:** The Calendar Round combines the Tzolkin with the Haab in a 52 solar year cycle. Each unique day in this calendar has four glyphs that read left to right. A number glyph precedes the Tzolkin day glyph, next a number glyph precedes the Haab month glyph. The most important day in the Calendar Round is 4 Ajaw 8 Kumk'u, the first day of the present creation.

The 52 year Calendar Round cycle is complete when, for instance, the combination of 4 Ajaw 8 Kumk'u repeats. The length of this process becomes clear when one observes that the immediate days following 4 Ajaw 8 Kumk'u are named 5 Imix 9 Kumk'u, 6 Ik' 10 Kumk'u, 7 Ak'bal 11 Kumk'u, etc. It requires the appearance of a special day (called the chief year bearer) in the Tzolkin calendar to inaugurate a Calendar Round cycle. The current K'iche Calendar Round concludes in 2026.

For all practical purposes, the Tzolkin, Haab, and Calendar Round served the needs of the Mayans. The Venus round of 104 years (two Calendar Rounds) was factored in for added divinatory possibilities. This calendar system, as interpreted by shaman/day keepers, covered every conceivable aspect of the spiritual and temporal life of the Mayans. No question too large or too small could fail to be divined according to the auguries associated with each particular day in the Calendar Round.

At 52 years, the Calendar Round was long enough for the vast majority of Mayans because life expectancy was less than 52 years. Likely seen only once in a lifetime, the end of a Calendar Round was an occasion for hope and dread. Fortunately, the New Fire ceremony at these endings has thus far ushered in successive new Calendar Rounds.

However, one element in Mayan society needed something more. In order to mark their place in time, Mayan kings and other noble personages instituted the Long Count.

**Long Count:** The Long Count is an era based concept that can stretch time over thousands of years either into the past or the future (actually even to infinity). There is little if any divinatory purpose to the Long Count. It tends to "flatten out" time with a long linear dimension. This enables a Mayan king to trace his ancestry for hundreds and thousands of years back to the First Four Mother/Fathers, to the creation of humans. The Long Count provides a starting point against which any event during the duration of this creation may be fixed in time. Such a capacity comes in handy when carving stone monuments. The Long Count date could show when a king acceded to the throne as well as those before him. Period endings and personal dedications within the lifetime of a king were often set in context by their Long Count date.

According to Mayan mythology, we are living in the 4th Creation. The starting date of this Creation is known to a surprising degree of certainty. In the 16th century CE, the notorious Bishop Diego de Landa burned the sacred writing of the Yucatec Maya, which, he said, "...they regretted to an amazing degree." Even so, de Landa had made notes of Mayan glyphs in his search for their alphabet. He was off on this count but his notes later become crucial to the correlation of Mayan calendar dates with the present day Gregorian calendar. Hundreds of years after de Landa it could be seen that the Mayan 4th Creation date 0.0.0.0.0 4 Ajaw 8 Kumk'u correlated with 11 August 3114 BCE.

Although the start of the 4th Creation is settled, the questions of when and why are more speculative. Munro Edmonson's conclusions may be the most satisfactory. He thought that the Long Count was inaugurated in 355 BCE, basing this on several calendar intervals falling on this date. He also thought that the Long Count was "predictive". That is, the Mayans decided to "end" the present Creation on winter solstice in 2012. They then backdated 13 baktuns (the length of a Great Cycle, a complete Creation period) to 11 August 3114 BCE. This provided the beginning and end of the 4th Creation:

0.0.0.0.0  4 Ajaw 8 Kumk'u to 13.0.0.0.0  4 Ajaw 8 Kumk'u.

The Long Count 4th Creation date is read left to right as: zero baktuns, zero katuns, zero tuns, zero uinals, zero kins (on a day called) 4 Ajaw 8 Kumk'u. The conclusion of the 4th Creation is read as: 13 baktuns, zero katuns, zero tuns, zero uinals, zero kins (on a day called) 4 Ajaw 8 Kumk'u. These dates appear interchangeable as both beginning and ending.

In calculating a Long Count date, a kin = one day, a uinal = 20 days, a tun = 360 days, a katun = 7,200 days, a baktun = 144.000 days.

To obtain these numbers: a kin is multiplied by 20 for 1 uinal; a uinal is multiplied by 18 for 1 tun; a tun is multiplied by 20 for 1 katun; a katun is multiplied by 13 for 1 baktun. Higher numbers are possible but apparently seldom if ever used.

With this system, any event in the present Creation could be definitively fixed. One simply counted the number of days that elapsed since the Creation date and added the Calendar Round date on which it fell. The Calendar Round date was not superfluous but rather the foundation of time on which the Long Count could stand.

To paint a quick portrait of the Long Count in action, recall the sad, sad story of 18 Rabbit, the 13th ruler of Copan. On a good day for 18 Rabbit, he acceded to the throne of Copan on 9.13.3.6.8 7 Lamat 1 Mol. That is 19 baktuns, 13 katuns, 3 tuns, 6 uinals, 8 kins or about 3809 years after the start of the 4th Creation. The Gregorian calendar date is 9 July 695 CE. 18 Rabbit had a fabulous reign, though often troubled, for over 40 years.

On 9.15.6.8.13 (January 738 CE), 18 Rabbit dedicated ball court 111A at Copan. Merely 107 days later on 9.15.6.14.0, 18 Rabbit had a terrible day. Kawak-Sky of Quirigua captured the gods of 18 Rabbit (meaning 18 Rabbit's Standard was taken in battle). Then 6 days after capture, 18 Rabbit was sacrificed at Quirigua on

9.15.6.14.6  6 Cimi 4 Zec (3 May 738 CE). All of these dates were, in due course, handily carved on stone monuments.

The basic purpose of the Long Count was to serve kings like 18 Rabbit and Kawak-Sky by placing their lines of ancestry and seminal life events within the framework of Mayan creation. Although, lesser nobles could also avail themselves of the Long Count if they wished to dedicate a new house, etc.

The story of the Long Count might end here. There is no indication that the Mayans are overly concerned with 13.0.0.0.0  4 Ajaw 8 Kumk'u (21 December 2012). It is an opportunity for thoughtful change.

However, the phenomenon of 2012 still looms in the air. Is there more to 2012? The winter solstice of 21 December continues to attract a plethora of fantastic scenarios of doom. For reasons of brevity as well as sanity, the cosmic Apocalyptic cataclysms "foretold" for 2012 will be set aside. There are several other interesting theories but one concept especially bears examination because it arises from the Mayan calendar itself, at least from the Long Count calendar.

Did the Mayans choose to end this Creation on 21 December 2012 because it marks a 26, 000 year cycle for our sun in its epic journeys through the Milky Way galaxy? Is there a special wisdom or shift in consciousness intended for us at this conjunction of the stars? John Major Jenkins believes so.

John Major Jenkins is the originator and leading proponent of the Galactic Alignment Theory. He has suggested that Mayan astronomers possessed the requisite knowledge to perceive that our sun would cross the Milky Way's center (the Dark Rift) on a path repeated once every 26, 000 years. That unique ecliptic passage of the sun through the Milky Way will occur on 21 December 2012. Jenkins believes that the end of the Mayan 4th Creation was chosen because of this unique conjunction. In Jenkins view, this reveals a Mayan mythology of World Ages. The 4th Creation of about 5125+ years combines with the first three Creations. So 4 x 5125+ = (almost) 26, 000 years. Winter solstice 2012, therefore, is a super conjunction of World Ages.

For Mayan astronomers to have calculated this 26, 000 year cycle, they must have understood the precession of the equinoxes. This would require a very difficult series of astronomical observations over long periods. Accuracy would be extremely hard to maintain. The precession of the equinoxes has been described as a "wobble" in the earth's rotational axis. The course of the "wobble" is followed from equinoxes to solstices. A complete "wobble" takes 26, 000 years.

Jenkins has his detractors, notably the above referenced Anthony Aveni. Jenkins and Aveni have had a running battle on this issue in their books The 2012 Story (Jenkins) and The End of Time (Aveni).

Aveni and Jenkins spar over several points, in particular, the site of Izapa in southern Mexico. Jenkins offers drawings and fuzzy photos of the sky to support his contention that the alignments of monuments at Izapa prove that the Mayans understood precession and the 26, 000 year cycle. Aveni counters with fuzzy photos of his own and says that Jenkins' contentions are not proven.

Suffice it to say that these books eventually conclude and the reader must weigh who has made the best argument. On balance, the higher probability lies with Jenkins. Aveni actually seems to do more to shore up Jenkins' theory than to debunk it. When he began his critique, Aveni acknowledged that Jenkins' proposition seemed reasonable on the surface. And during his critique, Aveni described in detail how the Mayans might have known about precession. He added that the Chinese were aware of precession in roughly the same era. When all was said and done, Aveni concluded that the Mayans might have understood precession but that it was not proven in the record.

Aveni seems unconvinced of his own position. The probabilities remain with Jenkins. The Mayans likely knew of precession. The choice of the 2012 end date is most probably not a mere coincidence. Even though the timing of the phenomenon may be imprecise by days, months or perhaps years, the 26,000 year cycle was intended to be manifest in the Long Count calendar.

Having said that, the next question is: So What? Not in the sense of who cares. But in the sense of : What if anything does it mean?

Did the Mayans see the Milky Way Galaxy as the World Tree? Will the sun's passage cross the Galactic Center, the Dark Rift, the womb of life, in a path taken 26,000 years ago. Do the Mayans mean for us to see and be renewed? Is it a general invitation?

I think there is enough evidence to lend support to these notions. There is reason to treat this coming moment as one full of possibilities. If one wishes to.

\* \* \* \* \* \*

Now, after a breath and meditative pause, we continue to the end of the Popol Vuh. The remaining pages take us to several new mountain homes, describe the magical and military prowess of particular lords, and conclude with naming the generational sequence of K'iche lords. The story tapers off but these final points are absolutely critical to status in K'iche society.

\* \* \* \* \* \*

# New Citadels

The time came when the wives of the first mother-fathers died. Not long after that, the K'iche left Hacavitz and settled on a mountain called "Place of Thorns" where they stayed for a lengthy time. Growing more numerous, the K'iche sought another home and arrived at a mountain named "Beard". This was in the fourth generation when Lord Sweatbath reigned. There were few quarrels in these days. Arrangements for marriages were made with handshakes over food and drink. It was then they began building with lime and plaster, stones and mortar.

At Beard, the K'iche decided to make a show of their glory, their authority. They displayed their "Shield" as a demonstration of their sovereignty. This angered the Ilocab, a neighboring tribe. They made war against Lord Sweatbath and the K'iche. But the K'iche crushed the Ilocab. Many captives had their hearts cut out before Lord Sweatbath and the Gods. All the tribes were in fear and awe at the sight.

As the K'iche clans and great houses grew in glory, they sought another citadel. They found a mountain called Rotten Cane, "place of reed fields". At Rotten Cane, the K'iche became even more numerous, crowded, and in the end, quarrelsome. They haggled about the price of their daughters in marriage. In arguments, they disturbed the bones of their ancestors. This was resolved in part by dividing the K'iche into nine lineages. Scores of palaces were built in Rotten Cane to house the many lords. Houses for the Gods were built. The true majesty of the K'iche was shown in the construction of the palaces and the painting of the surfaces.

None of this could have happened, though, were it not for the work of thousands of vassals. And the vassals were neither lured nor kidnapped. They rightfully "belonged" to the lords. The vassals held their lords in high esteem and celebrated their lords birthdays.

## Comment

What could be more prosaic? Throughout the ages, the discreet charm of the nobility has been: war, sacrifice (victims), feasting a victory, and quarreling about marriage arrangements. The K'iche were no different. And what price for a daughter? In the beginning, a handshake over food and drink. But as the fiery majesty of the kingdom rose, so did the price of a good marriage.

The temples (houses of the Gods) and palaces for the lords that were built in stone, covered in lime stucco, and richly decorated evoke the most impressive images of Mayan civilization — the dramatic, magnificently adorned ceremonial centers of Mayan cities. Even after abandonment and centuries of neglect, the partially restored monuments of stone entrance the visitor into a silent state of wonder. What must have been the effect in their heyday? And, of course, the loyal vassals sang happy birthday to the lords! Perhaps as long as the king and lords put on a good show and interceded successfully with the Gods, it seemed to work. But when people starved and wars were lost, it didn't work. The earlier example of 18 Rabbit is a case in point.

# The Essence of Lordship

In the fifth generation, Lord Gucumatz (Quetzal Serpent, Plumed Serpent) reigned as Ahpop (chief councilor, keeper of the mat).

Lord Gucumatz possessed the greatest degree of shamanic prowess of any K'iche lord in any generation. His essence was true spirit, true genius. For seven days, he rose to the sky. For seven days, he traveled to Xibalba. For another week, he became a serpent. Another time, an eagle. Then he became a jaguar. For seven days, he became just a pool of blood. All the lords and vassals feared Lord Gucumatz.

In the sixth generation, Lords Quicab and Cavizimah ruled the K'iche. These were lords of true military genius and power. They destroyed and conquered the neighboring tribes, the Rabinal, the Cakchiquel and others. If a town did not bring tribute to the K'iche, Lord Quicab struck terror in them and forced them to pay tribute. By the side of one town, a pile of stones was left as a reminder of Quicab's military power. Everyone who walked by the stones saw the sign of Quicab's manhood.

Sentries were dispatched to fortify and guard the towns that had been captured. These sentries engaged in further military feats and took spoils. They were given military titles and made the heads of new lineages.

K'iche kings and lords were marvelous in their essence, in their being, in every generation because they could see whether there would be war or death or famine or strife. The lords had a place to see these things. It was a book, the Popol Vuh. And the towns brought wonderful gifts of tribute to the K'iche lords: precious stones, bracelets, jade, silver, blue feathers, quetzal feathers. Also, the lords were very busy with the hearing of countless petitions from their vassals. They cried their hearts out in prayer for their people. They fasted for days and weeks in penance. They remained in the house of God, alone, with no women. The four highest lords carried the most responsibility. In pairs, they bore the lament of their people before the Gods. This was the happy price of lordship.

## Comment

The juxtaposition of Lord Gucumatz in the fifth generation and Lords Quicab and Cavizimah in the sixth underlined the ideal qualities of Mayan lords. The manifestation of true genius was the shamanic skill of Lord Gucumatz and the military power of Lord Quicab. They were the essence of manhood and the picture of emulation for the K'iche. The final step in the transition to a full fledged warrior culture came with the estabishment of the military lineages, in effect, a standing army and colonizing force. The sentry soldiers received their titles, their cushions, their seats. The police power of the state ruled supreme.

The luxurious tribute that the K'iche lords commanded from their defeated neighbors would seem to speak for itself. But the authors of the Popol Vuh wanted to make sure that the lords were not seen simply as profligate hoarders of gems and quetzal feathers. With the privileges of office, there came tremendous responsibilities. For those lords who took their public service seriously, there must have been a great deal of fasting, penance, personal bloodletting, and soulful prayers to the Gods on behalf of their constituents. For those who did not take their public duties to heart, there was (no doubt) a secret tunnel from the temple to the back door of the local pub.

# Naming the Generations

Naming the generations begins at the root, the first four mother-fathers. They were there when the sun, moon and stars showed themselves. Balam-Quitze was the root of the Cavecs. Balam-Agab was the root of the Greathouses. Mahout (Not Right Now) was the root of the Lord K'iches. Iqi-Balam had no sons.(For this summary, it is enough to list the Cavec lineage.)

Here are the "faces" of those who ruled the Cavecs. They are named in pairs, those who were Ahpop and Ahpop-Qamha in each generation. Sometimes the offices were held by one person.

Balam-Quitze, root of the Cavecs.
Qocavib, second generation.
Balam-QoNache,third generation.
Lord Sweatbath and Iztayul, fourth generation.
Gucumatz and Cotuha, fifth generation.
Tepepul and Iztayul, sixth generation.
Quicab and Cavizimah, seventh generation.
Tepepul and Iztaub, eigth generation.
Tecum and Tepepul, ninth generation.
8 Vines and Quicab, tenth generation.
Vucub-Noh and Cauutepech, eleventh generation.
3 Deer and 9 dog, twelfth generation. (Pedro de Alvarado invaded)
Tecum and Tepepul, thirteenth generation. (subject to the Spanish)
Don Juan de Rojas and Don Juan Cortes, fourteenth generation.

Thus, these are the lords who were Ahpop and Ahpop-Qamha of the Cavecs from the first generation to the present. (The authors went on to name the sequence of lordships for the Greathouses and the Lord K'iches.) Also, there were three Nim-Chocoh (Masters of Ceremony), one each for the Cavecs, the Greathouses, and the Lord Quiches. These three made pronouncements. They were highly respected "mothers of the word, fathers of the word".

Here, the story ends. The authors conclude:

There used to be a book, "still lost", that cannot be seen. Nonetheless, all has been told about the K'iche, now called Santa Cruz.

## Comment

The political motivation for the writing of the Popol Vuh is the naming of the lines of lords. The entire story is a wonderous tale of the cosmos but the life of the nation rides on who is in charge. Getting it right is a matter of life and death.

The Popol Vuh is obviously an idealized mythology of how things happened and how they should happen in the future. There are discrepancies in the generational sequences. It is not cut and dried. In fact, the strict lines of primogeniture were stretched almost beyond recognition at times. One translator said that these principles were honored mainly in the breaching. Even so the mythology survived.

******

We have arrived at the end of the Popol Vuh. All has been told. It was an astounding journey from the watery stillness, to the rising of the earth plain, the fate of the false sun, the attempts at the human work, the magic dances of First Father and the Hero Twins, the making of humans, the birth of the Four Mother/Fathers, the dawning, the travels and travails of the people born in the light. Now there is once again a book, a place to see. The lost eyesight has been restored.

Hopefully, the unacknowledged, underlying meaning of the Popol Vuh has also surfaced. That is: the "boys" usurped the magic of Blood Moon, built their sacrificial blood ballgame around that magic, and framed the blood rituals within Grandmother's sacred count of days. All of this was done in order to support kingship. Furthermore, by sympathetic extension, the Mayan Cosmic Ballgame is related spiritually to our ballgames. Our competitive ballgame culture is a spiritual child of the Mayan warrior ballgame culture.

However, I can not "prove" the connection. I can only suggest. It's a ballplayer's leap. You jump or you don't. You're more or less inclined. If one does not sense the connection by now, nothing that I can offer is likely to result in a blinding flash of light. But, perhaps my further musings may suggest associations that have not thus far come to mind.

# Summer, Fall, Winter, Spring

In the United States, baseball is a spring/summer sport. Football is a fall sport. Basketball is a winter sport. They tend to overlap a bit but this is how the seasons go. Someone wins, someone loses. Seasonal champions are crowned. In the end, though, it does not matter who wins or loses, who has the bragging rights for the year. It matters only that the games are played. The earth's path around the sun, the wheel of the year, the seasonal changes are marked by these ballgame rituals. Football, basketball, and baseball are the cosmic rituals, the collective story that holds the country together. No one says this must be. There is no sacred text proclaiming it. It is so simply because in fact, in practice, in custom, it is so.

Hope springs eternal when winter recedes. New buds appear. Baseball practice begins. Everyone is equal. The infield diamond is swept clean. The outfield grass is mown. The bases are secured. The pitcher's mound is tended. Home plate is brushed off. The batter steps up. The pitcher delivers. Then, for the following five to six months, the contest continues on playgrounds, in schools, in professional leagues. The culmination, the apogee is the World Series of Major League Baseball, the "Fall Classic" as it is called.

As a child, I played baseball but it wasn't my main sport. I did not try out for the high school team. Yet rainy, chilly days in April brought the spring rebirth of my hometown Syracuse Chiefs of the Triple AAA, International League, only one level below Major League Baseball. Throughout the 1950s I scrounged the money for a bleacher seat to watch Syracuse play the Havana Cuban Sugar Kings - a crackerjack baseball squad. Then for some reason in 1959, the Cuban team no longer came to Syracuse.

Of course, it is said that baseball is just a game, a pastime. But baseball is actually a creation story. Baseball is the ritual re-enactment of building the universal house of creation. It creates a place for the human community on earth. The three bases and home plate are the cardinal directions, the four posts of the universal house. The pitcher's mound is the navel of the world, the center post, the beginning. The game may progress incrementally but a home run is its most dramatic stroke. In one swing of the bat, the ball (seed of life) is sent into the cosmos, beyond the field of play. As the batter makes a home run trot round the bases, the universal house is constructed in one fell swoop. A player who hits many home runs is highly prized. The description of New York's Yankee Stadium as "the house that Ruth built" has a deeper meaning. Conversely, players who are seen to have unfairly enhanced their chances of hitting home runs are despised because they sully the creation story.

In the dog days of August, an occasional breath of fall may come on the air. By the time crisp cool temperatures induce the riotous colors of the fall foliage, football season is well begun. Lazy hazy days of Summer give way to bone crushing tackles on American gridirons. Football was my first love.

In a scruffy playground at the end of Frisbee Court in the public housing projects where I grew up, I was a favorite target of the passer in touch football games as we moved the ball downfield toward the tree that marked the goal line. Standing by the tree, I would gaze up the hill, past the Upstate Medical Center, to Syracuse University's Crouse College of Art which sat like a medieval castle overlooking the housing projects, the city, and Onondaga valley to the south. From its height, Syracuse University called me. Never was this call so strong as during football season.

On S.U. football home game days, my friends and I climbed the hill heading to Archbold Stadium, a concrete oval that could seat forty thousand around a grass gridiron. We waded through fallen leaves and tossed smooth, rich brown horse chestnuts at each other along the path of our climb. When we reached the stadium, there was a rush of adrenaline since the first order of business was to sneak-in to the game. Buying a ticket was out of the question for us urchins from the housing projects. We circled the stadium for opportunities to sneak-in. If the volunteer ushers in orange hats looked the other way, we scaled the chain link fence, scooted up the concrete wall, and squeezed through the iron bars that ringed the oval. Once in, mingling with the crowd, I was entranced by the roar of the beanie capped frosh, the pungent smell of cigars and whiskey, the smoke of the touchdown cannon, the beauty of the college girls, and the clash of players on measured grass. In a reference to the salt industry that gave Syracuse its sobriquet "Salt City", the college band belted out the fight song, "The Saltine Warrior is a bold bad man and his weapon is a pigskin ball." It sent shivers up my spine. In the 1940s, the university marching band was comprised of One Hundred Men and a Girl. Invariably, the "Girl" was a solidly built, high strutting, baton twirling, long haired beauty. Though I could not articulate it, even then my young body sensed that she was the symbolic heart of the spectacle.

Football is a continuation of the yearly creation story that baseball began. Football's story lies in the underlying symbols of the game. The symbols are simple, few and in plain view. On a precisely delineated lengthy rectangular field, opposing players face off over a vulva shaped ball. The "offensive" team has "possession" of the ball. Play generally begins when the "center" of the offensive team lifts the football from a stationary position on the ground and passes it between his legs to a player in the "backfield" behind him. The football is now "live". It must proceed at a satisfactory rate "downfield" through the opposing "defensive" team. The goal for the offensive team is to retain physical possession of the football while forcing it past the defensive team and into an area called the end zone. This is a "touchdown". Alternatively, the offensive team may kick the football through the goalposts at the back of the end zone for a "field goal".

A process of impregnation is the symbolic core of football. Relentlessly, the offensive team pushes the football down the playing field, the birth canal, to be touched down in the sacred earth, planted in the end zone or to enter the holy temple between the high posts, the stylized upright legs, the portal to the womb. The defensive team's task is to intercept, to steal, to dislodge, to thwart the passage of this fertile seed by any means. On both sides of a mythical line of scrimmage, very large men run at full speed and deliberately crash into one another, quite often with injurious results. If a defensive team stops the offensive team, then they go on "offense". Football's long march back and forth, up and down the birth canal concludes in early winter with the National Football League's "Super Bowl".

In December, the snows come to Syracuse, turning fall to winter. The lakes freeze. Sometimes we went ice fishing. But I didn't go in for winter sports like skating or skiing. Winter meant indoor basketball. The big game in town when I was a kid was the Syracuse Nationals of the original National Basketball Association (later they moved to Philadelphia). I saw George King sink two free throws against the Fort Wayne Zollner Pistons at the Onondaga County War Memorial auditorium in 1952 to win Syracuse's only NBA title. Basketball was my best sport. I played on my high school team and on my college team in freshman year. I could have played on the varsity team in college but my life gravitated toward sixties politics — the civil rights and peace movements. In the end, I probably played my best basketball in federal prison from 1968-70 when I was doing time for draft card burning. Who can forget the game in the slammer when I scored forty-eight points?

Today basketball is high paced and high scoring but that was not true at its foundation. It was more calculated. The basketball (bouncing head, seed, planet, star) would infrequently pass through the hoop (the circle and net portal to the underworld) in the early days. Yet in the quickened present, there is still a sense of deep penetration, sleep, resting as this heavenly body soars through space to find its narrow entrance to eternity. The ball game creation story of basketball connotes winter death before the ball in another form once again rises in spring. The do or die single elimination tournament of the NCAA college teams in "March Madness" seems to elicit more excitement than the later finals of the National Basketball Association professional teams.

In April, there is baseball.

******

That's it. That's all there is. I don't mean to disappoint. Or to minimize. It really is as simple as I have made it. The ballgame dance with the earth, sun, moon, and stars is the oldest sacred story. It is the universal story at this very moment. There are other stories, belief systems, religions but they are covers for the ball game cycle. The underlying energetic force of human culture is driven by and expressed in the cyclic rituals of the ball games of creation.

In America, it happens that baseball, football, and basketball provide the essential ritual format for the ball game cycle. In the rest of the world, the rolling head or seed is primarily found in soccer. Unlike the American World Series of baseball or the Super Bowl of NFL football, the soccer World Cup is truly a worldwide event. Every country in the world has a theoretical chance through a series of competitions at being in the World Cup. Soccer, the "beautiful" game, is beautifully simple in its play and symbolism. The game is fast, furious, and free flowing. The fate of a country and the world hangs on who slips the ball into the sweet womb of the net. For me, an affinity and understanding of soccer came late in life when I lived in England for four years in the 1970s. Besides following English soccer, I even played in pick-up games with my English workmates. With my good basketball hands and ball playing savvy, I was quite useful as a goalkeeper. I was hopeless though at controlling the soccer ball with my feet. My ball skills were acquired long before soccer's rise in popularity in the United States. And although interest in soccer has increased in this country, I cannot see that soccer would ever approach the hold that football, basketball, and baseball have in American culture.

There are obvious differences between the Mayan ballgame of creation and the American ballgame creation cycle but the differences are cosmetic rather than substantive. The Mayan creation story is fully articulated and acknowledged. It's a story seen in the sky, that unfolds over thousands of years. There are texts written and painted on walls of stone. The players are human and divine. The story is understood to be meaningfully critical to Mayan life.

The American ballgame creation cycle exists in a state of utter denial. Every aspect of its cosmic, sexual, and political import is unacknowledged. It's dismissed as a mere game. It can be understood only by following its seasonal paths, peering beneath its symbols, and noting the values it teaches. The Mayan ballgame supports the warrior life. The American ballgame cycle supports competition and conquest. The imagery is filled with slam dunks, bone jarring hits, mowing down of the opposition, and the humiliation of the enemy. These sentiments carry over wholesale to infuse the culture's economic and political relations with ballgame metaphors.

Some maintain that the American ballgame story encourages the development of "teamwork" skills and that many ball teams function like a "family". But this highly dysfunctional family model is structured on the authoritarian hierarchy of a coach's decisions and the goal of one family team to crush another family team. And a player on such a family team who does not meet expectations or is injured will soon be shown the door. A compassionate family is not the goal. As past United States president, General Dwight D. Eisenhower, observed, "...the true mission of American sports is to prepare young people for war."

The Mayans know that the ballgame dance must always be. The stars, sun and moon will pass again and again. The corn will grow and die and grow again. The American ballplayers also know that the ballgame dance is eternal and unavoidable although they would not admit it. The problem we face (besides denial) lies in the nature of the dance. Men control a ritual, a universal dance that is skewed, out of balance. The dance is confrontational, not flowing or forgiving or compassionate or communitarian. Bodies are weapons, instruments of force.

Why is this our dance? How did it happen? Why do we allow it? Can the dance be shifted?

******

I think that shamanic error has skewed our balance. Like the Olmec and Mayans, shamans across the world stole the Moon.

Far back into the early Paleolithic, shaman/scientists had a varity of methods for predicting lunar and solar eclipses. Shadow casting techniques made use of sticks, hands, leaves and shining jewels. These methods were accurate enough to be useful and later evolved into more accurate methods.

It's not necessary to detail these techniques. The point is that they offer reasonable ways in which a proto-scientific astronomy delveloped from very ancient times and culminated in an intermediate stage of astronomical observation at sites like Stonehenge, Chaco Canyon, the Temple of Poseidon, and

Mayan temples. For example, the Dresden Codex (a Mayan bark document that survived the Spanish) was a prediction table (not actual observations) that did not miss one of the 77 partial or total solar eclipses from 755 to 788 AD.

The popular science writer William Calvin made an instructive comment about the social/religious significance of early eclipse prediction, "... this is a limited story about how predictive science might have originated via imperfect methods, it may also be one of the stories about how primitive religions arose and were sustained by their apparent success in predicting or manipulating the heavens ... the emergence of powerful leaders with specialized knowledge ... may have been the shamans who seemed to have such power over the sun and moon because they'd figured out a method of eclipse prediction - and likely kept it a secret among themselves."

Ah, yes. Therein lies the error. The shaman stole the moon and used it for personal advantage — influence, prestige, privilege, acqustion. The loss or misuse of shamanic vision was the error in ancient times and continues to this day.

To spell it out, the shamanic error is a ballplayer's error. For the shaman is a ballplayer. He (as the game became his) juggled the Moon across the horizon and through the night sky. He was there when she rose, when she changed shapes, when she moved the tides. He knew her rhythms and was there to catch her. His feet danced upon the mother ball (herself a daughter of the stars) as she spun through the dark, sparking skies. The great ballplayer, One Hun-Ahpu, claimed the magic of Blood Moon in the underworld. Through her, he lived again in his ball playing sons. After the sons resurrected the father, one became the sun, the other the moon.

Shamans continue to play ball in modern times. We no longer need them to predict eclipses or to see patterns in the sky. That job is done by scientists, professional astronomers. However, our shaman/ballplayers remind us who owns the ball, who controls the game, who marks the time. Some modern shamans (notably those of the world religion, soccer) do have an innate sense of the nature of the ball. The Uruguayan writer, Eduardo Galeano, quoted a Brazilian soccer shaman from the 1950s named Didi, He, Didi, spoke of the ball in feminine terms, "I always felt a lot of affection for her. Because if you don't treat her with affection, she won't obey. Sometimes she'd go one way and I'd say: 'Come here child', and I'd bring her along. I'd take care of her blisters and warts and she'd always sit there, obedient as can be. I'd treat her with as much affection as I give my own wife. I had tremendous affection for her. Because she's fire. If you treat her badly, she'll break your leg. That's why I say: 'Boys, come on, have some respect. This is a girl that has to be treated with a lot of love ... Depending on the spot where you touch her, she'll choose your fate."

Our shaman priests of football, basketball, and baseball do know that the games must be played. Football must climax in the Super Bowl. Basketball in March Madness. Baseball in the World Series. In this way, the seasons turn, the heros rule for their moment and the cosmos is safe for another year.

It is clear, though, that a shift is needed in the game plan. In ballgame parlance, we need to make several half-time adjustments. The present strategy, with roots in a past almost too distant to comprehend, is not working for us. We need to huddle up. All of us. Every sentient being on earth and throughout the universe. The earth herself. The heavenly bodies. The dark space in between. Everything and no thing that is aware of itself. Nothing will be missing. Even nothing.

Time itself can be misleading. Shamanic error cannot simply be ascribed to an origin in the past. Time is linear, cyclic, and in the moment. We hold these three within us. Shamanic error has always been and will always be possible in every moment.

However, since we appear to be mere humans, perhaps we should anthropomorphize the equation. Let us dance a ballgame dance where the singing garden boys and the ballgame warrior boys accommodate rather than confront. Where the song is sung and the war is sidestepped. Self interest and social justice are not incompatible. Science and Spirit are not incompatible. Though it will take a clever dance to hold the balance. It might be called a new dance but it is simply a dance so old that it looks like new.

2012 will come and go. Baseball, football and basketball seasons will come and go and return next year, unless our species succeeds in its own extinction. In that case bacteria will have to find other hosts to continue the game.

If an "original sin" has been commited in the Long Count of hominids on earth, it is best understood as an "original theft". Economic oppression, faith based evil bogies, and the "natural" inevitability of warfare arise from an original and on-going theft of blood magic.

We can meet on the hill, dance with the moon, sun and stars, restore the blood magic. That's the dance I would like to see. Our freedom and well being depend on such a dance.

I hope the "boys" come to dance. I mean the Hero Twins, Hun-Ahpu and Xbalanque. They are good boys. They let me see my nature more clearly. I play ball, therefore I am alive. I am alive, therefore I play ball. I would love to see the boys dance the Armadillo, the Poor-Will.

Anthony Aveni should come too. When I read the final paragraph of the epilogue to his book, he immediately vaulted to the top of my New Age guru list. The enlightened Mayan day keeper who Aveni suggested had put the Mayan calendar together remains lost in the past. But recently Aveni bumped into a live Mayan shaman at a conference on Hieroglyphics. He queried this shaman on 2012. The Mayan answered, "Only the cycle will end. Time will continue, and we will learn to live in peace and harmony, for we are all a part of a plan to help the gods complete the creation and perfection of the world." Aveni concluded, "..I definitely approved of his message. All of us have a role to play. The life of our planet has always depended on us and the actions we take here on earth."

Since Aveni's sentiment is substantially similar to those seeking wisdom, higher consciousness, harmony, and oneness with nature, are we on the same page?

# Ballad of 2012

Just in case. If all else fails. If the doomsayers begin to prevail. If the end appears nigh. It would be best to have a spell in place. I would not be much of a honky tonk witch if I did not have a spell at the ready. The Mayans have their songs and do not need any more. But to ward off cataclysm, we should have a song that works as a spell.

The spell will be successful only if everyone is singing. As a honky tonk witch, I will know who is singing and who is not. Please do your part. Don't let the world end. Any style or arrangement is fine as long as it's Country.

## Ballad of 2012

*(warrior boys your day is done,*
*  the singing garden boys have come)*
*Hear the tale of Hunahpu*
*Brother Xbalanque too*
*All along the Milky Way*
*A great ballgame they did play*
*(a great ballgame they did play)*

*One was sun*
*One was moon*
*Earth and stars*
*Danced to their tune*
*(earth and stars danced to their tune)*

*They played a game of sacrifice*
*Cut out hearts with their knife*
*Blood Moon's heart was the ball*
*She who gave life to all*
*(she who gave life to all)*

*They stole her heart*
*The Queen of Night*
*To use in ballgame sacrifice*
*(to use in ballgame sacrifice)*

*For many many thousand days*
*The warrior boys had their way*
*But now the garden boys do say*
*In 2012 we'll have our day*
*(in 2012 we'll have our day)*

*The singing garden boys do say*
*In 2012 we'll have our day*
*(in 2012 we'll have our day)*

\* \* \* \* \* \*

Damn, the song is unfinished. Everyone will have to finish their own version. It needs a couple more verses. Put it out on the Net.

Remember, I'm listening.

# Bibliography

Arguelles, Jose, *The Mayan Factor* (Bear & Company, 1987)

Aveni, Anthony, *The End of Time* (University Press of Colorado, 2009)

Calleman, Carl Johan, *The Mayan Calendar* (Bear & Company, 2004)

Calvin, William H., How *The Shaman Stole The Moon* (Bantam, 1991)

Christenson, Allen J., (trans.) *Popol Vuh* (O Books, 2003)

Coe, Michael D., *The Maya* (Thames & Hudson, 1987)

Edmonson, Munro, (trans.) *The Book of Council: The Popol Vuh of the Quiche Maya of Guatemala* (#35 Middle American Research Institute, Tulane University, 1971)

Fash, William Scribes, *Warriors and Kings, The City of Copan and The Ancient Maya* (Thames & Hudson, 1991)

Freidel, David; Schele, Linda; and Parker, *Joy Maya Cosmos* (William Morrow, 1993)

Galeano, Eduardo, *Soccer In Sun and Shadow* (Verso, 1998)

Gillette, Douglas, *The Shaman's Secret* (Bantam, 1997)

Jenkins, John Major, *The 2012 Story* (Jeremy P. Tarcher/Penguin, 2009)

Markman, Roberta & Peter, *The Flayed God* (Harper/Collins, 1992)

Miller, Mary Ellen, *The Art of Mesoamerica from Olmec to Aztec* (Thames & Hudson, 1986)

Morley, Sylvanus G., *The Ancient Maya* (Stanford University, 1946)

Pinchbeck, Daniel, *2012, The Return of Quetzalcoatl* (Tarcher/Penguin, 2006)

Recinos, Adrian, (trans.) *Popol Vuh* (English version from Spanish by Delia Goetz and Sylvanus G. Morley, University of Oklahoma Press, 1950)

Rice, Prudence M,. *Maya Calendar Origins* (University of Texas Press, 2007)

Scarborough, Vernon L., and Wilcox, David R. (eds.) *The Mesoamerican Ballgame* (University of Arizona Press, 1991)

Schele, Linda and Miller, Mary Ellen, *The Blood of Kings* (George Braziller, 1986)

Schele, Linda and Freidel, David, *A Forest of Kings* (William Morrow, 1990)

Schele, Linda and Mathews, Peter, *The Code of Kings* (Simon & Schuster, 1998)

Spence, Lewis, (trans.) *Popol Vuh* (David Nutt, Long Acre, London, 1908)

Stephens, John L., *Incidents of Travel in Central America, Chiapas, and Yucatan, Vol. 1 & 2* (Dover Publications, 1969)

Tedlock, Dennis, (trans.) *Popol Vuh* (Simon & Schuster, 1996)

Tedlock, Dennis, *2000 Years of Mayan Literature* (UC Press, 2010)

van Akkeren, Ruud W., *Authors of the Popol Vuh* (Ancient Mesoamerica, 14 (2003), 237-256)